Frommer's

100

Places to Take Your Kids
Before They Grow Up

1st Edition

by Holly Hughes

WILEY

Wiley Publishing, Inc.

Contents

Published by:

Wiley Publishing, Inc.

111 River St.
Hoboken, NJ 07030-5774

ISBN 978-0-470-43896-1

Editor: Jennifer Polland
Production Editor: Heather Wilcox
Photo Editors: Richard Fox & Jennifer Polland
Interior book design: Melissa Auciello-Brogan
Production by Wiley Indianapolis Composition Services

Front cover photo: Child on sand. © Tom Bol/Aurora Photos/AGE Fotostock, Inc.
Back cover photo: Niagara Falls. © Maciej Korzekwa/iStockphoto

For information on our other products and services or to obtain technical sup-port, please contact our Customer Care Department within the U.S. at 800/762-2974, outside the U.S. at 317/572-3993 or fax 317/572-4002.

Wiley also publishes its books in a variety of electronic formats. Some content that appears in print may not be available in electronic formats.

Manufactured in the United States of America

5 4 3 2 1

About the Author

Holly Hughes has traveled the globe as an editor and writer—she's the former executive editor of Fodor's Travel Publications, the series editor of Frommer's Irreverent Guides, and author of *Frommer's New York City with Kids*, 10th Edition. She's also written fiction for middle graders and edits the annual *Best Food Writing* anthology. New York City makes a convenient jumping-off place for her travels with her three children and husband.

An Invitation to the Reader

In researching this book, we discovered many wonderful places. We're sure you'll find others. Please tell us about them, so we can share the information with your fellow travelers in upcoming editions. If you were disappointed with a recommendation, we'd love to know that, too. Please write to:

Frommer's 100 Places to Take Your Kids Before They Grow Up, 1st Edition
Wiley Publishing, Inc. • 111 River St. • Hoboken, NJ 07030-5774

An Additional Note

Please be advised that travel information is subject to change at any time—and this is especially true of prices. We therefore suggest that you write or call ahead for confirmation when making your travel plans. The authors, editors, and publisher cannot be held responsible for the experiences of readers while traveling. Your safety is important to us, however, so we encourage you to stay alert and be aware of your surroundings. Keep a close eye on cameras, purses, and wallets, all favorite targets of thieves and pickpockets.

A Letter from the Author

Why These 100 Places?

The obvious question just about everybody asked me when I told them I was writing this book: "Have you been to all 100 places?" I regret to say I haven't—not yet—but I've been to a surprising number of them over the past few years. If not, I've talked to other families who have generously shared their travel memories with me. Immersed in writing this book, at times I almost imagined we had been everyplace. But I have to say, now that it's written, I'm glad we haven't seen it all and done it all yet—we still have a few traveling years ahead of us as a family, and now we've got a thicker file than ever of thrilling trips to look forward to.

Of course, choosing a destination is only part of the challenge. Knowing what it's like to travel with youngsters, I've tried to give you the tools you need to make these trips unforgettable. I've dug up tidbits of history or other background, so you can look like experts when you're leading your children around a site. It's not enough just to go to a place—you've got to imagine how the people of this distant era lived, why one army won this battle and not the other, what makes this park different from that one, which animals thrive where. You do it to keep the kids interested, and then somehow you find yourself having a richer experience of the place, too. Awakening that sense of wonder is what travel is all about, for adults as well as children.

I've also suggested strategies for certain destinations—whether or not to hire a tour guide (some enrich the experience, others bog you down in boring details); whether to drive, walk, or take the tram; whether to dawdle over a museum's every exhibit or zero in on a few key displays. With the proper strategy, you'd be surprised how much even young children can delight in these destinations. Don't sell them short! The payoff is all cumulative—the more your children travel, the more they'll observe and appreciate on further trips, and the more intriguing trips you'll be able to plan.

Of course, you are the experts when it comes to knowing your own family's interests—whether that be history, culture, nature, outdoor adventure—so rather than follow a geographic scheme, I've organized this book in groups of destinations with a similar emphasis, spread around the globe. After a successful trip to one destination, I hope you'll consider planning new trips to others in that category—chances are you'll like them too.

The geographic index in the back will help you match nearby destinations, so you can take in a whole cluster of sights on one vacation.

A Note on Hotels

I wish I'd had space to give you full-blown hotel reviews, but you can rely on these choices being the most family-friendly lodgings in the area. Traveling with a family is not cheap, so I tended to recommend moderately priced hotels rather than the most expensive lodgings. (You don't need my help in finding the poshest hotel in town—what's hard to find is the small hotel with no advertising budget.) I also recommend modern, plainly furnished hotels rather than antique-laden B&Bs, which, for all their charm, may not welcome children. The other criteria I look for: kitchenettes, room service, room lay-outs that accommodate extra beds, TVs in the room, and the trump card, a swimming pool (give us a good pool and my kids will accept almost any-thing). Price ranges of course are relative. The three price ranges I note— $$$ (expensive), $$ (moderate), and $ (inexpensive)—don't conform to one set of dollar equivalents, but reflect the local market. A $125-per-night motel room in South Dakota would seem expensive, but if you can find something clean and safe at that price in New York, snap it up. For fuller descriptions (and other useful travel info), please consult the corresponding Frommer's guides for these destinations.

Age Ranges

For each destination, I've also indicated an age range for children. When I say "All ages," that means you could bring a baby or young toddler in a stroller and not feel out of place. I'm not saying the 6-month-old would get much out of the experience (!), but at least you could take older siblings there without the baby being a hindrance. In a few cases, I've upped the age range on a destination if it somehow poses challenges handled best by older kids. I admit that these recommended age ranges are subjective—for lack of a more objective test, I've based them on what my own children would have been interested in at what age. My kids have become good travelers over the years. Yours can be too.

They're only young once, so see the world through their eyes—you won't regret it!

Other Great Guides for Your Trip:

Frommer's Icons

We use four feature icons to help you quickly find the information you're looking for. At the end of each review, look for:

ⓘ   Where to get more information

✈   Nearest airport

🚆   Nearest train station

🛏   Recommended kid-friendly hotels

Frommers.com

Now that you have this guidebook to help you plan a great trip, visit our website at **www.frommers.com** for additional travel information on more than 4,000 destinations. We update features regularly to give you instant access to the most current trip-planning information available. At Frommers.com, you'll find scoops on the best airfares, lodging rates, and car rental bargains. You can even book your travel online through our reliable travel booking partners. Other popular features include:

- Online updates of our most popular guidebooks
- Vacation sweepstakes and contest giveaways
- Newsletters highlighting the hottest travel trends
- Podcasts, interactive maps, and up-to-the-minute events listings
- Opinionated blog entries by Arthur Frommer himself
- Online travel message boards with featured travel discussions

Acknowledgments

Many thanks to all my fellow parents whose brains I picked for travel suggestions over the past two years. You were so generous with your trip memories, I almost felt in some cases as if I had traveled there with you. And to all the other parents who had to listen to my enthusiastic ramblings by the coffee urns at PTA meetings and on the soccer field sidelines—thank you for never letting your eyes glaze over as I raved on and on about yet another far-flung destination they really should visit.

I've also relied on the devoted corps of Frommer's writers to supply me with phone numbers, addresses, and recommendations of their own favorite family destinations. Your descriptions have been invaluable—you're the real experts in your various parts of the world, and I'm beholden to you.

And finally, I have to thank my husband and children, who not only put up with having Mom disappear into her office for hours at a time but who are the best travel companions I could ever ask for. I've been blessed with three children who are great travelers—they love getting up before dawn to catch an early plane, they know how to amuse themselves on long flights, they can negotiate a crowded train platform, they don't need to be pacified with videos on long car trips, and they are excited every time we check into a new hotel. They make travel an adventure to look forward to.

—Holly Hughes

Monument Valley
The Iconic Wild West Landscape
Ages 6 & up • Kayenta, Arizona

WHEN MOST OF US THINK OF THE AMERICAN WEST, THIS IS WHAT clicks into our mental Viewmasters: A vast, flat sagebrush plain with huge sandstone spires thrusting to the sky like the crabbed fingers of a primeval Mother Earth clutching for the heavens. Ever since movie director John Ford first started shooting westerns here in the 1930s, this landscape has felt familiar to millions who have never set foot here. We've all seen it on the big screen, but oh, what a difference to see it in real life.

If you possibly can, time your visit to include sunset—as the sheer walls of these monoliths capture the light of the setting sun, they

Monument Valley.

truly seem to catch fire. There are three ways to tour the area, which is also a Navajo reservation: driving the 17-mile Valley Drive, hiking with a guide, or horseback riding. Guides are usually local Navajos, born and bred to this barren landscape. If you drive, you can take your own car; but it is a rocky, rutted dirt road, so I personally would opt for a **jeep or van tour.** (Hold out for one that visits backcountry areas that are otherwise off-limits to visitors, including close-ups of several **natural arches** and Ancient Puebloan **petroglyphs.**)

Sticking to the **Valley Drive** takes you to **11 scenic overlooks,** once-in-a-lifetime photo ops with those incredible sandstone buttes for backdrop. Often Navajos sell jewelry and other crafts at the viewing areas, or even pose on horseback to add local color to your snapshots (a tip will be expected).

John Wayne—John Ford's favorite leading cowboy—roamed these scrublands on horseback, and seeing it from a Western saddle does seem like the thing to do. Local outfitters run everything from a guided 1-hour trail ride to an overnight campout. One of the most comprehensive tour companies (jeeps, hikes, horses, you name it) is **Sacred Monument Tours** (© 435/727-3218; www.monumentvalley.net), but plenty of other operators can be booked from the visitor center. Although most of the park lies in Arizona, it is right on the state border, and you enter it from Utah. Just outside the park, **Goulding's Museum and Trading Post** is furnished as it was in the 1920s and 1930s when the moviemakers first discovered the area; there are also displays about the many films that were shot here.

Be sure to get a map so the kids can learn the eccentric rock formations' names—imaginative names like the Mittens, Three Sisters, Camel Butte, Elephant Butte, the Thumb, and Totem Pole. And as you stare at them, take an extra moment to imagine the forces of nature that have sculpted the soft desert stone into these incredible shapes. It's an only-in-America panorama that the kids won't ever forget.

ⓘ U.S. 163, 30 miles north of Kayenta (© **435/727-5870;** www.monumentvalleyonline.com)

✈ Flagstaff Pulliam, 200 miles

🛏 $$$ **Goulding's Lodge,** Monument Valley, UT (✆ **435/727-3231;** www.gouldings.com). $$ **Hampton Inn Kayenta,** U.S. 160, Kayenta, AZ (✆ **800/HAMPTON** or 928/697-3170; www.hampton-inn.com).

WHY THEY'LL THANK YOU: Just like the movies—only more so.

2

Awesome Vistas

The Redwood Forests of California

All ages • Crescent City, California

IT'S HARD TO EXPLAIN THE FEELING YOU GET IN THE OLD-GROWTH forests of **Redwood National and State Parks.** Everything seems big, misty, and primeval—flowering bushes cover the ground, 10-foot-tall ferns line the creeks, and the smells are rich and musty. It's so *Jurassic Park* you half expect to turn the corner and see a dinosaur.

The scientific name for these massive conifers is *Sequoia sempervirens,* cousins of the giant sequoias (see Sequoia National Park ❸). Sheathed in rough reddish bark, miraculously fire-resistant, their stout straight trunks shoot up 100 feet or more before a canopy of branches begins; they often reach a total height of more than 300 feet. Among the planet's most ancient individuals—the oldest dated coast redwood is more than 2,200 years old—they only grow in temperate rainforests, meaning nowhere but the U.S. Pacific Coast. In 1968, the federal government created Redwood National Park (nowadays combined with three state redwood parks) to protect what's left of this seriously endangered species. The relative isolation of this stretch of coast helped the forests survive intact, but it also makes for a long drive.

The most spectacular display is along the **Avenue of the Giants,** a 33-mile stretch of U.S. 101 through the Humboldt

Redwoods State Park (© **707/946-2263;** www.humboldt redwoods.org). Environmentalists bemoan the tacky attractions along this route, but youngsters love 'em—from south to north, hollow **Chimney Tree,** where J. R. R. Tolkien's Hobbit is rumored to live; **One-Log House,** a small dwelling built inside a log; and the **Shrine Drive-Thru Tree.** More dignified landmarks include **Founders Grove,** honoring those who started the Save the Redwoods League in 1918; and the 950-year-old **Immortal Tree.** Don't settle for looking at all this out your car window—from many parking areas you can ramble on short loop trails into awesome redwood groves.

The other cluster of parks begins another 100 miles or so farther north, threaded along U.S. Highway 101. The most scenic drive parallels 101, along the **Newton B. Drury Scenic Parkway,** passing through redwood groves and meadows where Roosevelt elk graze, and **Coastal Drive,** which has grand views of the Pacific. But again, the truly spine-tingling experience requires getting out and hiking through these soaring perpendicular woods. Pick up a park map to find your way to **Tall Trees Trail,** a 3¼-mile round-trip to a 600-year-old tree often touted as the world's tallest (get a permit at the Redwood Information Center in Orick); the self-guided mile-long **Lady Bird Johnson Grove Loop;** the short, very popular **Fern Canyon Trail;** or, for the littlest hikers, the quarter-mile-long **Big Tree Trail,** a paved trail leading to—what else?—a big tree.

ⓘ U.S. 101 (© **707/464-6101;** www.nps.gov/redw)

✈ Crescent City

🛏 $ **Curly Redwood Lodge,** 701 Redwood Hwy. S. (U.S. 101), Crescent City (© **707/464-2137;** www.curlyredwoodlodge.com). $$$ **Lost Whale Inn,** 3452 Patrick's Point Dr., Trinidad (© **800/ 677-7859** or 707/677-3425; www.lostwhaleinn.com).

WHY THEY'LL THANK YOU: Seeing the redwoods before they're gone.

Sequoia & Kings Canyon National Parks
Giant Trees of the Sierras
All ages • Visalia & Fresno, California

ONLY 200 MILES BY ROAD FROM OFTEN-OVERRUN YOSEMITE NATIONAL Park, Sequoia and Kings Canyon national parks still feel like untrammeled wilderness. Only one road, the **Generals Highway,** loops through the area, and no road traverses the Sierra here. High-altitude hiking and backpacking are what these parks are really all about; some 700 miles of trails traverse this terrain of snowcapped Sierra Nevada peaks (including **Mount Whitney,** which at 14,494 ft. is the highest point in the lower 48 states), high-country lakes, and alpine meadows. For families, though, there's one main attraction: the largest groves of giant sequoias in the Sierra Nevada.

Though they are two separate parks, Sequoia and Kings Canyon are contiguous and managed jointly from the **park headquarters** at Ash Mountain—you hardly know when you're leaving one and entering the other.

Of the 75 or so groves of giant sequoias in the parks, the two most convenient to visit are Grant Grove (in Kings Canyon near the Big Stump park entrance), and Giant Forest (in Sequoia, 16 miles from the Ash Mountain entrance). In **Grant Grove,** a 100-foot walk through the hollow trunk of the **Fallen Monarch** makes a fascinating side trip. The tree has been used for shelter for more than 100 years and is tall enough inside that you can walk through without bending over. In **Giant Forest,** the awesome **General Sherman Tree** is considered the largest living thing in the world; single branches of this monster are more than 7 feet thick. Other trees in the grove (each of them saddled with names like General Lee or Lincoln) are nearly as large, creating an overall effect of massive majesty. Giant Grove has some 40 miles of intersecting footpaths to wander; the 6-mile **Trail of the Sequoias** will take you to the grove's far eastern end, where you'll find some of the finest trees.

While Sequoia's raison d'être is those incredible trees, Kings Canyon encompasses the deepest canyon in the United States: Drive to **Road's End** on the Kings Canyon Highway (open late May to early Nov) to stand by the banks of the Kings River and stare up at granite walls rising thousands of feet above the river.

ⓘ **Ash Mountain entrance,** CA 198 from Visalia. **Big Stump entrance,** CA 180 from Fresno, CA (☏ **559/565-3341;** www.nps.gov/seki, www.sequoia-kingscanyon.com, or www.visitsequoia.com).

✈ Fresno-Yosemite, 53 miles

🛏 $ **Dorst Campground,** in Sequoia near Giant Forest (☏ **800/365-2267**). $$ **Wuksachi Village & Lodge,** 64740 Wuksachi Way, Sequoia National Park (☏ **866/807-3598** or 801/559-4930 [international]; www.visitsequoia.com).

WHY THEY'LL THANK YOU: The redwoods' awesome (and even more endangered) cousins.

Best Things to Do in Sequoia & Kings Canyon National Parks

- **See the world's biggest tree;** walk in the Giant Forest to see this and many other giants.
- **Hike along the Kings River** in a canyon meadow or up into the granite high country.
- **Tour Crystal or Boyden Cave** to see weird rock formations and branching passages and to experience total darkness.
- **Swim in river pools** where Native Americans bathed in the foothills near the Ash Mountain entrance.
- **Backpack** or take a horse-packing trip into true mountain wilderness.

The Brooklyn Bridge
New York Icon
All ages • New York, New York

AS THRILLING A SIGHT AS THIS BEAUTIFUL BROWN-HUED EAST RIVER bridge is from afar, with its Gothic-style towers and lacy mesh of cables, the view from the bridge is even more thrilling. A boardwalklike **pedestrian walkway** goes all the way across, raised slightly above the car traffic. One mile long, it should take about half an hour to traverse—except you'll be tempted to stop more than once to ooh and ahh at the vision of Manhattan's skyscrapers thrusting upward, with the great harbor and Verrazano Bridge beyond.

The Brooklyn Bridge took 16 years to build, from 1867 to 1883, and for a while, it seemed to be cursed—original designer, John A. Roebling, died from tetanus contracted when his foot was crushed while surveying the site, and his son, Washington, who took over the job, fell ill with the bends after diving into the river to supervise the workmen laying the pilings. A virtual invalid afterward, Washington Roebling watched the bridge going up through a telescope from his house in nearby Brooklyn Heights, while his wife actually supervised much of the completion of the project.

Why has the Brooklyn Bridge captured the popular imagination more so than other New York City bridges? Well, for one thing, it was the first steel-wire suspension bridge in the world when it opened in 1883. (Until then, the only way to get from Manhattan to Brooklyn was via ferry.) Ever since, the Brooklyn Bridge has become a byword in New York lore. The standard old joke defines a con artist as a guy trying to sell rubes the deed to the Brooklyn Bridge. Cocky teenage hoodlums have proved their bravado by shinnying up its cables, and suicides with a flair for the dramatic have plummeted to their deaths from those same cables into the tidal currents below. The bridge has appeared in countless movies and TV shows, its outline practically synonymous with New York City.

From Manhattan, the **entrance ramps** are along Centre Street just south of Chambers Street on Park Row; pedestrian ramps on the other side empty out into Brooklyn's downtown—a bit of a wasteland on weekends, but not a far walk from **Brooklyn Heights,** one of the loveliest brownstone neighborhoods you'll ever see. Go armed with a map. If your kids aren't hardy urban trekkers, walk halfway to get the view and then double back to Manhattan. Be aware that things get awfully windy once you're above the water!

(i) ✈ ⊨ For information on New York City, including airport and lodging, see Manhattan **14**.

WHY THEY'LL THANK YOU: It's one thing to see a landmark, another to walk across one.

Beautiful Bridges **5**

Crossing the Golden Gate Bridge

Ages 6 & up • San Francisco, California

WARN THE KIDS AHEAD OF TIME THAT THE GOLDEN GATE BRIDGE IS not golden at all, but a flaming orange. (As toddlers, my kids thought it was going to be made of actual gold.) Once past that surprise, though, they cannot fail to be bowled over by this glorious bridge spanning the Pacific Ocean where it meets San Francisco Bay. In all lights it has a magical quality—brightening at dawn, glowing at sunset, glittering at night, or blazing proudly through the city's trademark fog. It's one of those quintessential U.S. landmarks, familiar from dozens of movies. Cars roll over it, boats cruise under it, and airplanes buzz overhead, but this bridge is best experienced while walking.

The Golden Gate Bridge.

This deeply gouged strait was named the Golden Gate after the area's golden brown hills, yet it is a triply apt name when you also consider San Francisco's boom in the 1849 Gold Rush and its role as America's western gateway for immigrants. Though it echoes the East Coast's Brooklyn Bridge, built 54 years earlier, the West Coast bridge has a streamlined Art Deco look, with its gracefully swung single span, spidery bracing cables, and subtly tapering twin towers. Given the strong tides and depth of the strait, skeptics had claimed for years that a bridge could not be built here—that it would buckle in a gale wind or collapse in an earthquake. Nevertheless, construction began in May 1933, creating jobs for thousands for 4 years at the height of the Depression, and was completed at the then-colossal cost of $35 million. (Its East Bay sibling, the 8¼-mile-long Oakland Bay Bridge, was completed the year before.) With only one pier actually planted in the water, it features a single long central span, designed intentionally to sway in the strait's winds. At 1¾ miles long, it was for 27 years the longest suspension bridge in the world; its twin towers soar 746 ft., and its two main cables weigh 11,000 tons apiece.

On its opening day in 1937, some 200,000 pedestrians joined an inaugural walk across the bridge. To make your crossing, bundle up against the wind, then set out from the **Roundhouse** on the east side of the bridge. Be prepared: The traffic alongside the pedestrian walkway gets pretty noisy, and the bridge vibrates. Even if you only make it halfway, the experience is amazing; walk all the way to **Vista Point** in Marin County and you'll be rewarded with one of the most famous cityscape views in the world.

(i) Hwy. 101 N from San Francisco (www.goldengatebridge.org)

✈ 🏨 See the Cable Car Hills of San Francisco ㉒.

WHY THEY'LL THANK YOU: A high-wire walk they'll never forget.

The Lighthouse Tour of Maine

All ages • Kittery to Castine, Maine

IT'S ONE OF THOSE CLASSIC IMAGES OF NEW ENGLAND: THE STALWART lighthouse, perched above crashing waves, sending out its beam to welcome home the fishermen. And nowhere is the concentration greater than in Maine. It's only natural—Maine's jagged coastline is so fringed with inlets and islands and carved-out bays, if a giant came along and pulled it straight it would be 5,500 miles long. You need a lot of lighthouses to navigate a shore that crazy, and driving from one to the next is a great connect-the-dots way to enjoy the state.

Start out north of Kittery, turning off Route 1 to York Beach. At the northern end of Long Sands Beach, postcard-perfect **Nubble Light** sits high on a peninsula, with its white Victorian keeper's house alongside. On a clear day, if you've got binoculars, you may also be able to see slim granite-gray **Boon Island Light** 10 miles out to sea—New England's tallest lighthouse, at 13 stories high. Just north of Kennebunkport, off Route 1 on Maine 208, the hamlet of Cape Porpoise has a lighthouse offshore on **Goat Island,** which has been used by the Secret Service detail to protect the senior President Bush when he's at his Kennebunkport home.

There are no fewer than five lighthouses in greater Portland— from south to north: the gracefully proportioned **Cape Elizabeth Light** at Two Lights State Park, featured in the paintings of Edward Hopper; the tapering white **Portland Head Light,** Fort Williams Park, 1000 Shore Rd., an active lighthouse since 1794 with a small museum in its former keeper's house; the granite-block **Ram Island Ledge Light** offshore from Portland Head; the fire-hydrant-shaped **Spring Point Light** on a breakwater at the end of South Portland's Broadway; and around the same point, the **Portland Breakwater Light,** nicknamed Bug Light for reasons the kids should be able to figure out.

Go north on I-95 to Brunswick, where Route 1 branches off east, running like a spine along the heavily indented coast. In Boothbay Harbor, ferries from the pier visit the stout white **Burnt Island Light,** which you can tour. In Bristol, there's the whitewashed stone **Pemaquid Point Light,** which now contains a fishing museum. In Port Clyde, the peaceful **Marshall Point Light,** which also contains a small museum, played a bit part in the movie *Forrest Gump*. Northeast of here, the Penobscot Bay area has a host of lighthouses, including a pair on either side of Rockland harbor, the quirky **Rockland Harbor Southwest Light,** North Shore Rd., growing out of a wood-shingle house, and the red-brick **Rockland Breakwater Light** on the north side of the harbor. Another 50 miles or so on Route 1 will take you around the top of the bay to Castine, where the privately owned rough, conical **Dice Head Light** sits at the end of Route 166.

ⓘ **Maine Office of Tourism** (ℂ **888/624-6345;** www.visitmaine. com)

✈ Portland International, 45 miles from Kittery, 140 miles from Castine

🛏 $$$ **Sebasco Harbor Resort,** 29 Kenyon Rd., Sebasco Estates, near Brunswick (ℂ **877/389-1161** or 207/389-1161; www. sebasco.com). $$ **Topside,** 60 McKown Hill, Boothbay Harbor (ℂ **877/486-7466** or 207/633-5404).

BEST TIME: Spring, or fall, when you can enjoy the foliage. In summer Rte. 1 backs up for miles.

WHY THEY'LL THANK YOU: Watching the beacon light wink on and off.

7 **Drives**

San Juan Skyway: Million-Dollar Highway

All ages • Begins & ends in Durango, Colorado

CLOSE TO THE FOUR CORNERS, WHERE COLORADO, UTAH, ARIZONA, and New Mexico meet at right angles, this 256-mile loop of highway is one of the country's most spectacular drives, taking in the whole panorama of the Southwest—from ancient Native American cliff dwellings to Wild West towns to smart ski resorts, all against an incredible backdrop of 10,000-foot-high Rocky Mountain passes, canyons, waterfalls, and alpine meadows.

I prefer to follow the circuit clockwise from Durango, saving the most breathtaking scenery for the end. You can drive it in 1 day, but there are enough intriguing stops en route to make it worth 2 or 3 days. For example, the first (and, frankly, least scenic) 45 miles, along U.S. 160 west from Durango, takes you past **Mesa Verde National Park,** an awe-inspiring archaeological site with thousands of Ancestral Puebloan cliff dwellings that deserves a full day on its own. Ten miles past the park, just before the town of Cortez, turn north on CO 145 up the Dolores River Valley, slicing into mountains thickly forested with green. Sixty miles past Dolores, the kids should be able to spot the startling rock spire that earned **Lizard Head Pass** its name. A few miles past here, you can detour 4 miles east to historic **Telluride.** This is where Butch Cassidy robbed his first bank, in 1889. The museum at 201 W. Gregory Ave. (© **970/728-3344**) displays loads of artifacts from the town's Wild West Days, and you get a distinct late 1800s vibe just from walking around the landmarked downtown streets.

Colorado 145 goes west, following the San Miguel River Valley to Placerville, where you pick up CO 62 to head north over the Dallas Divide. You'll come next to **Ridgway,** a tiny old railroad town; go south on U.S. 550 to **Ouray,** another quaint Old West town to explore (a soak in the hot springs here makes a great break from

Packing for Planes & Cars

FOR A PLANE TRIP
Pack the following in your carry-on bag:

- The number of diapers your child wears in a day, plus an extra three
- A changing pad in case the tiny restroom in the airplane has no pull-out changing table
- A minimal number of toys—one coloring book and a stuffed animal will suffice
- Bottles for infants, sippy cups, and snacks for toddlers
- A goodie bag with surprises, such as a Discman with a CD of music or stories; books; or small plastic toys

FOR A CAR TRIP
Bring along the following to help your car rides go more smoothly:

- A cooler with drinks, snacks, fruits, and veggies
- A flashlight to help locate items that have rolled under your seat for the 10th time in the last 5 minutes
- Window shades for the sun
- Audiotapes of stories or children's songs.
- Consider a portable DVD between the two front seats so kids can watch videos
- Other items to consider bringing include a first-aid kit, a box of wipes for clean-ups, blankets, plastic bags for motion sickness, and a change of clothes. Always have a cellphone in case of emergencies.

driving). Past Ouray, you'll be driving the Million Dollar Highway, so named because millions of dollars passed over it in the great days of Colorado gold and silver mining. It's still worth a million dollars just for the views; the next 23 miles, over Red Mountain Pass to **Silverton,** are breathtaking, as the road shimmies up the sheer sides of a gorge, dives through tunnels, and passes cascading waterfalls. On the Red Mountain slopes around you, look for relics of mining equipment and log cabins. From Silverton, U.S. 550 climbs over two last passes, the Molas Divide and the Coalbank Pass; south of Purgatory, you join the gorgeous route of the Durango & Silverton Narrow Gauge Railroad as you head back to Durango.

ⓘ **Durango Area tourist office,** 111 S. Camino del Rio (℃ **800/525-8855;** www.durango.org)

✈ Durango/La Plata, 14 miles

🛏 $$ **New Sheridan Hotel,** 231 W. Colorado Ave., Telluride (℃ **800/200-1891** or 970/728-4351; www.newsheridan.com). $$ **The Strater Hotel,** 699 Main Ave., Durango (℃ **800/247-4431** or 970/247-4431; www.strater.com).

BEST TIME: Apr–Oct (passes may be blocked by snow in winter).

WHY THEY'LL THANK YOU: Million-dollar mountain vistas.

8 Drives

The Pacific Coast Highway
California's Oceanside Spectacle
All ages • Los Angeles to San Francisco, California

BEGINNING NEAR THE OLD MISSION TOWN OF SAN JUAN CAPISTRANO, state highway 1 hugs the California coast all the way up to Leggett, in northern California—and I mean it *hugs* the coast, darting around coves and clinging to steeply shelving cliffs, with the Pacific Ocean almost always out your side window. It's not the most efficient route to take from southern to northern California (or vice versa). Travelers intent on getting there fast opt for inland I-5, or at least U.S. 101. No, if you're driving the **Pacific Coast Highway,** you're looking for scenery—and some of the most spectacular coastal scenery in the world it is.

While some consider the PCH the whole series of connected highways from the Mexican border to Canada, I define it as California Highway 1 (which sometimes overlaps with U.S. 101). At various points, this winding two-lane road may be called the Cabrillo Highway, after the Spanish explorer, or El Camino Real, the old Spanish road linking a chain of early settlements. What really matters is its proximity to the Pacific.

We tend to skip the southern section, avoiding L.A.'s congestion, and start alongside the bleached sands of **Santa Monica Beach** 87. We usually break up the drive into 3 days so we can stop en route to walk on beaches, explore small towns, and so on. Along the way—say, around Cambria, near **Hearst Castle** 72— suddenly we're no longer in Southern California, and things get more rugged. Up near **Half Moon Bay,** there's a steep downward plunge of the road called **Devil's Slide** that the kids love. Past San Francisco, we cruise a lonelier stretch of Northern California coast, where we make a pilgrimage to the giant redwoods—depending on time, we may make it as far as Muir Woods or **Redwood National Park** 2.

The most dramatic stretches of the drive occur where the mountains crowd close to the ocean's edge—for instance, just north of Santa Barbara, where the Santa Inez peaks tumble precipitously to the beach, or the entire section from Morro Bay north to Carmel, where the sea nips at the toes of the Santa Lucia mountains. Each curve you whip around reveals another jaw-dropping vista, narrow strips of white foam-edged sand purling below you on one side, furrowed brown mountainsides beetling over you on the other. Surfers bob on their boards offshore—or are those seals?—and hawks coast dreamily overhead. It's beautiful at noon, with blue skies and bright sun; it's beautiful in a haunting fog; it's beautiful glowing at sunset; it's even beautiful in a wistful gray rain. It's just plain beautiful.

I've driven the Pacific Coast Highway twice with my kids, both times going south to north. Next time I plan to drive it north to south, which I suspect is even more thrilling. Maybe in a red convertible, with the Beach Boys' "Wouldn't It Be Nice" blasting from the car radio . . . ah, California.

ⓘ www.visitcalifornia.com. www.us-101.com.

✈ Los Angeles International. San Francisco International.

🛏 See Hearst Castle **72**.

WHY THEY'LL THANK YOU: Riding the curves, watching the surf.

---

⑨ Boat Rides

The Seattle-Victoria Ferry
Sailing the High-Speed Puget Cats
All ages • Seattle, Washington, USA, to Victoria, British Columbia, Canada

CROSSING THE U.S.-CANADA BORDER IS GENERALLY A FAIRLY ROUTINE experience—but not if you sail across it on a **high-speed catamaran** from Seattle, Washington, to Victoria, British Columbia. The trip takes only 3 hours, just enough time for the kids to roam around the boat, get a bite to eat, and stare out the windows at the gorgeous northwest coast. Exciting as open water is, it soon gets monotonous for children; one of the glories of this trip for kids is that most of the ride is on glacier-carved **Puget Sound,** where land can be viewed on either side, the rugged conifer-mantled highlands of the Olympic Peninsula on one side and the rural Skagit Valley on the other.

You leave from Seattle's busy ferry port, Pier 69, with the futuristic Space Needle lifting its curious head over the downtown Seattle skyline and majestic Mount Rainier visible to the south, snowcapped

The Seattle-Victoria ferries.

even in summer. Working your way past Seattle harbor's sailboat and kayak traffic, you'll enter convoluted Puget Sound, with the mountains of the Olympic Peninsula gradually rearing their peaks on your left. Coming out of Puget Sound near Port Townsend, you'll see the lovely San Juan Islands on the right (the same company runs ferries to the San Juans, including some whale-watching excursions). Then it's across the Strait of Juan de Fuca, the first stretch of open water on your voyage so far.

On the far side of that strait lies Vancouver—Vancouver Island, that is, which is not the same thing as the mainland city of Vancouver. What is on Vancouver Island is British Columbia's capital, Victoria, which is like a little slice of Victorian England served up on the northwest coast of North America. Ferry schedules are organized to make a day trip perfectly doable, with plenty of time to explore Victoria before heading back to Seattle. The mild Pacific climate is beautifully suited to horticulture, and Victoria's pride and joy is its rose gardens, particularly the spectacular **Butchart Gardens,** 800

Benvenuto Ave., Brentwood Bay (© **250/652-4422;** www.butchart gardens.com). If you can't sell your kids on visiting a garden, there's plenty to see around the charmingly restored Inner Harbour: **Miniature World** in the Fairmont Empress Hotel, 649 Humboldt St. (© **250/385-9731;** www.miniatureworld.com), with loads of small-scale dioramas from history and literature, the glass-enclosed views of harbor creatures in the **Pacific Undersea Gardens,** 490 Belleville St. (© **250/382-5717;** www.pacificundersea gardens.com), and the **Victoria Butterfly Gardens,** 1461 Benvenuto Ave., Brentwood Bay (© **250/652-3822;** www.butterfly gardens.com), which are exactly what the name says.

ⓘ © **800/888-2535** or 206/448-5000 or 250/382-8100; www. clippervacations.com

✈ Seattle-Tacoma International, 23km (14 miles). Victoria International, 26km (16 miles).

🛏 $$ **Admiral Inn,** 257 Belleville St., Victoria (© **888/823-6472;** www.admiral.bc.ca). $$$ **The Edgewater,** Pier 67, 2411 Alaskan Way, Seattle (© **800/624-0670;** www.edgewaterhotel. com).

WHY THEY'LL THANK YOU: Gliding up the fjord in time for tea and scones.

10 **Boat Rides**

Cruising the Mighty Mississippi
A River Ride Through the Heart of America
All ages • Various locations along the Mississippi River

THE NATIVE AMERICANS LIVING ON ITS SHORES CALLED IT THE MESSIPI, or "big river," but in American lore the Mississippi River is so much more. Yes, it is long—at 2,350 miles, it's the third-longest river in the world—but as it surges north to south down the middle of America, it gives this continent a heartbeat that is essentially, uniquely ours. I vividly remember the thrill of crossing it for the first time, at age 13, on a nighttime train, with a momentous feeling of Heading West. To ride its majestic brown waters, for whatever stretch of the river, is to feel connected to West and East and North and South all at once. And if you're going to do it, do it the right way, on a **steam-powered paddle boat** with lacy white fretwork and fluted smokestacks and the whole banjo-strumming shebang.

Several river towns offer 1- or 2-hour paddle-wheel cruises to give you a taste of what it feels like to be out on that great river—St. Paul, Minnesota; La Crosse, Wisconsin; St. Louis, Missouri; Tunica Resort, Mississippi; and New Orleans, Louisiana all have sightseeing paddle-wheelers. From LeClaire, Iowa, you can even book a 2-day cruise on the *Riverboat Twilight* along the Upper Mississippi to Dubuque and back (© **800/331-1467;** www.riverboattwilight. com). To really give the kids that old-timey thrill, though, a longer trip is the way to go, to see how the river changes character over its course. The headwaters begin up in Minnesota at Lake Itasca, but the Mississippi is merely a small stream at that point; after it meets the Minnesota River at St. Anthony Falls, it widens significantly, with steep bluffs on either side. Just above St. Louis it joins up with the Illinois and then the Missouri rivers, becoming truly huge and fast-moving. As it rolls down into Arkansas and Louisiana, the softer soil of the Delta creates a mazy, loopy river course, with many islands and a lazy majesty all its own. By the time it reaches New Orleans, the Mississippi has really *been somewhere.*

The **Delta Steamboat Company** rules the river when it comes to these extended journeys: It has three vintage paddle-wheelers with sleeping cabins, theaters, dining rooms, and even a swimming pool; a "riverlorian" on board tells stories of the river, and young passengers can hang out in the pilothouse and earn a cub pilot's license. Itineraries vary according to which river ports you choose, from Minneapolis to St. Louis to Memphis to New Orleans. The boats dock at charming river towns along the way, with guided tours arranged; between ports, take along a copy of *Huckleberry Finn* or *Life on the Mississippi* and plunk yourself down in a deck chair while the kids scamper around the ship. A week on the river—it's a great way to see America in microcosm, exploring it at the pace of another century.

ⓘ ☏ **800/510-4002**; www.mississippirivercruises.com

✈ Depends on port of embarkation

🛏 On board

WHY THEY'LL THANK YOU: Rolling down the river.

---

11   **Boat Rides**

Scouting Alaska's Inside Passage
Ferries to the Glacier
All ages • Juneau, Alaska

EVERY SUMMER, BOATLOADS OF TOURISTS CROWD ONTO LUXURY cruise ships to be pampered on their way through Alaska. But that's not my idea of a rugged wilderness experience—not when you can still travel in comfort on the swift, well-outfitted ferries of the **Alaska Marine Highway System,** with the option of planning your own itinerary to suit your family's interests.

Officially designated an All-American Road, the Alaska Marine Highway covers 3,500 nautical miles from Bellingham, Washington, out to the Aleutian Islands. A fleet of sleek blue-hulled ferries steams its entire length, but I think the most interesting segments are those of the Inside Passage, that crazy network of inlets and channels around the countless islands of the Alaskan Panhandle. Squeezed between the Canadian Yukon and the Gulf of Alaska, this little strip of southeast Alaska—a breathtaking mix of dense green northwest rainforest and pristine white glaciers—stretches 500 miles from Ketchikan to Yakutat.

In the middle is Juneau, Alaska's capital city and where you'll probably arrive by plane. Before leaving Juneau, trundle the kids off to see the **Mendenhall Glacier,** Glacier Spur Road (© **907/789-0097**), where you can stand in front of a wall of blue ice and feel its chilly breath. The two destinations that most interest my kids are in opposite directions from Juneau: **Ketchikan,** a spruced-up logging town with the world's largest collection of totem poles that's 17 hours south by ferry; and **Sitka,** an exotic mix of Russian and Tlingit cultures that's 8¾ hours north of Juneau by ferry. The beauty of taking the ferries? Using Juneau as a base and making separate excursions to Ketchikan and Sitka just takes planning. If you schedule it right, you may even be able to hit every town at an hour when the cruise mobs are gone and the locals relaxed.

Spending several hours on these ferries is no problem. These are handsome modern crafts, with restaurants, gift shops, and in some cases even movie theaters on board, not to mention solariums and observation lounges where you can park yourselves to watch the scenic coast roll past. Naturalists often come along for the ride to talk about Alaska's wildlife and geology with passengers; some ships have small video arcades or play areas for toddlers. For overnight journeys, you can reserve two- to four-berth cabins (book several months in advance for summer voyages), although you are also free to roll out your sleeping bags on the comfy reclining seats in the lounges. Hey, that counts as roughing it in my book.

ⓘ 6858 Glacier Hwy. (© **800/642-0066** or 907/465-3941; www.ferryalaska.com)

✈ Juneau International

🛏 $$ **The Driftwood Lodge,** 435 Willoughby Ave., Juneau (© **800/544-2239** or **907/586-2280;** www.driftwoodalaska.com). $$$ **Goldbelt Hotel Juneau,** 51 E. Egan Dr., Juneau (© **888/478-6909** or **907/586-6900;** www.goldbelttours.com).

WHY THEY'LL THANK YOU: Waking up to see a glacier slide past your window.

Atlantic City's Monopoly Streets

All ages • New Jersey

SINCE CASINO GAMBLING ARRIVED IN THE 1970S, THIS ONCE-PROUD Victorian seaside resort 60 miles east of Philadelphia has been reborn as the Vegas of the East Coast—decidedly a mixed blessing for families. The ghost of the old Atlantic City is still here, though, especially on the mile-long wooden **Boardwalk** that curves along the uncrowded white-sand beach. Food stands and arcades survive between the hulking casino properties, and visitors can take a nostalgic ride in old-fashioned rolling chairs. And to get kids interested, Atlantic City has a unique hook: It's one giant Monopoly® board.

This is the city that the "creator" of Monopoly, Charles Darrow, had in mind when patenting his game board in 1933. Actually, Darrow stole the game from an Atlantic City woman named Ruth Hoskins, who had invented it to play with friends (hey, it was the Depression, and Darrow was hungry). Hoskins had put her hometown's street names on her game board, and they're still here today. Atlantic City's street-naming scheme is fairly simple—parallel to the Boardwalk, avenues are named after seas and oceans (going inland, Pacific, Atlantic, Arctic, then low-rent Baltic and Mediterranean), while the cross-streets that connect them are named after states. Walk down the Boardwalk east to west from Vermont Avenue to Indiana Avenue and you may feel like you have turned into a shoe, or an iron, or a top hat, or one of the other classic Monopoly game tokens.

Along the way, you can sample Atlantic City's most kid-oriented attractions: the **Absecon Lighthouse** at Rhode Island Avenue (228 steps to a great shoreline view at the top); carnival rides and games at the renovated **Steel Pier** at Pennsylvania Avenue; a **Ripley's Believe It Or Not** at St. James's Place; and, farther west, the **Ocean One** shopping mall at Arkansas Avenue, and a **minigolf** course at Mississippi Avenue. Let the busloads of gamblers crowd inside the claustrophobic casinos: You're outside walking along the ocean, with sunshine, salt air, sea breezes, and a box of saltwater taffy. It's a fun and funky day at the shore.

We were puzzled, though, that we couldn't find Ventnor Place or Marvin Gardens—but that's because they aren't in Atlantic City at all, but in Margate, two towns south. (On your way, drive by **Lucy the Elephant,** 9200 Atlantic Ave., a huge wooden roadside curiosity from the 1880s.) **Marvin Gardens** was Charles Darrow's hasty misspelling of Marven Gardens, a charming 1920s-era subdivision off the 7400 block of Ventnor Avenue. It took a bit of detective work to drive down here and find those two missing streets, but that made our Atlantic City Monopoly quest all the more special.

ⓘ **Tourist Office,** 2314 Pacific Ave. (ⓒ **888/AC-VISIT;** www. atlanticcitynj.com)

✈ Atlantic City, 10 miles

🛏 $$ **Atlantic City Hilton,** Boston Ave. and Boardwalk (ⓒ **800/ 257-8677** or 609/347-7111; www.hiltonac.com). $$ **The Days Inn on the Boardwalk,** Morris Ave. and Boardwalk (ⓒ **609/344-6101;** www.atlanticcitydaysinn.com).

WHY THEY'LL THANK YOU: Finding Marvin Gardens.

Unique Cityscapes 13

Las Vegas: Cruising the Strip
Ages 6 & up • Nevada

Call it the Seventh Wonder of the Artificial World—in its own way, Vegas is every bit as amazing as the Grand Canyon. After a brief flirtation with being a family-friendly destination, Las Vegas has lapsed wholeheartedly back into its Sin City image, but even so, it's such an outrageous phenomenon, every kid should at least see it once.

The Las Vegas Strip at night.

Drink in the bizarre panorama first by cruising up and down Las Vegas Boulevard South, aka the Strip—traffic generally crawls, which should make it easy to see everything; if you don't have a car, view it from the new monorail, which will eventually run the length of the Strip. Do it once by day, spotting all the outlandish architecture; do it once again by night, when the competing dazzle of neon signs is simply breathtaking. Time things right so you can catch the Strip's free outdoor spectacles: the **dancing fountains** at the Bellagio, 3600 Las Vegas Blvd. S; the **exploding volcano** at the Mirage, 3400 Las Vegas Blvd. S., and the nightly **pirate battle** at Treasure Island casino, 3300 Las Vegas Blvd. S.

Several of the casino-hotels' lobbies are like mini-amusement parks, with stage-set scenery and themed shops and cafes: Just guess what cities are re-created at **Paris Las Vegas,** 3655 Las Vegas Blvd. S.; **The Venetian,** 3355 Las Vegas Blvd. S.; and **New York–New York,** 3790 Las Vegas Blvd. S. At the pyramid-shaped **Luxor,** 3900 Las Vegas Blvd. S., there's a full-scale reproduction of

King Tutankhamen's tomb, authentically handcrafted in Egypt; or, for all-out kitsch, visit the talking statues in the Forum Shops at the Roman Empire–themed **Caesars Palace,** 3570 Las Vegas Blvd. S. The **MGM Grand,** 3799 Las Vegas Blvd. S., has a multilevel glass enclosure where you can watch lions frolic; the **Mirage** has a mini-zoo of exotic cats and elephants owned by Siegfried & Roy, as well as a dolphin habitat; the **Imperial Palace,** 3535 Las Vegas Blvd. S., has a world-class car collection, many of them formerly owned by celebrities; and there are even theme-park rides built into some casinos. Most of these attractions are free, and even the ones that charge admission charge only a small amount.

There are fabulous shows to see at night, and splendiferous pool areas to lounge around. You can make day trips into the desert to the **Hoover Dam** 62 and the **Grand Canyon** 81. But when all is said and done, what the kids will remember is that nighttime view of the Strip. It's brilliant, it's brash, it's exotic, it's truly one of a kind. No city can out-Vegas Vegas.

ⓘ **Tourist office,** 3150 Paradise Rd. (ⓒ **877/VISITLV;** www. visitlasvegas.com)

✈ McCarran International

🛏 $$ **Mandalay Bay,** 3950 Las Vegas Blvd. S. (ⓒ **877/632-7800** or 702/632-7777; www.mandalaybay.com). $$ **MGM Grand,** 3799 Las Vegas Blvd. S. (ⓒ **877/880-0880** or 702/891-7777; www. mgmgrand.com).

WHY THEY'LL THANK YOU: Getting that neon fix.

14

Manhattan
A Kid-Sized Slice of the Big Apple
All ages • New York, New York

I WAS 13 THE FIRST TIME I VISITED NEW YORK CITY, AND I FELL IN LOVE with it at once, its quirkiness and energy and the sheer size of it. I'd walk around staring up at the impossibly tall buildings, gaping at images I'd seen in countless movies and TV shows. I couldn't wait to move here. But it wasn't until I had kids that I got to know the other New York, the one where *Spider-Man* fades out and *Stuart Little* takes over. This is the Manhattan I now know and love—let me give you the key to this city.

One of the secrets is not to spend your entire time in crowded, pricey Midtown. There are three must-see sights in Midtown: the view from the top of the **Empire State Building,** Fifth Avenue & 34th Street; the sunken plaza of **Rockefeller Center,** Sixth Avenue & 47th–50th streets, where an immense gold statue of Prometheus lounges over twirling ice skaters in winter and umbrella cafe tables in summer; and **Times Square,** 42nd Street & Broadway, with its dizzying razzmatazz of neon signs and theater marquees. (A fourth must-see if you've got 'tween girls: the **American Girl Place** doll store/theater/restaurant at 609 Fifth Ave.) But after that, get out into the neighborhoods.

New York is so densely packed, there's always something interesting on the next block, and then the next. Downtown is an example—once you've started your day with the ferry trip to the **Statue of Liberty and Ellis Island** 🔟, it's an easy stroll through the skyscraper canyons of **Wall Street** to the historic ships and shops of **South Street Seaport,** 12 Fulton St. Let yourselves wander ever northward, through the exotic scramble of **Chinatown,** the 19th-century tenements of **Little Italy,** the hipster loft district of **SoHo,** then the leafy brownstone streets of **Greenwich Village.**

New York Kids' Top Five Cheap Thrills

1. Ride in the front car of the subway train, standing at the front window to watch the train hurtle down the tunnel.

2. Stand on the street gratings above a subway line when the train comes thundering along underneath.

3. Run into the middle of a flock of pigeons, and make them all fly up at once.

4. In a skyscraper elevator, stand on tiptoe when the elevator starts to go up, and lower to a squat as you speed upward.

5. On the double-long accordion-style city buses, sit in the seats right in the hinge so you can swivel when the bus turns a corner.

Who needs to pay to go into tourist attractions, when you can shop and snack and explore a kaleidoscope of cultures?

The heart of New York for kids is **Central Park,** an 840-acre island of green between the apartment buildings of the Upper West Side and the Upper East Side. For one thing, it's bookended by New York's two greatest museums—the **American Museum of Natural History** **56** and the **Metropolitan Museum of Art** **65**, across the park from each other at 79th Street. Between museum visits, roam this brilliantly landscaped park, a seemingly natural countryside plunked down in the middle of the city. Near 65th Street on the east side, you can ride a vintage **carousel** and visit the **Central Park Wildlife Center;** midpark at 72nd Street is the **Lake,** with that elegant Bethesda Terrace you've seen in the movies. You'll see New York families jogging, biking, flying kites, throwing Frisbees, roller-skating, sledding, walking their dogs, playing in the playgrounds. Come join them.

The Empire State Building.

ⓘ **Tourist office,** 810 Seventh Ave. (ⓒ **212/484-1200;** http://nycvisit.com)

✈ John F. Kennedy International, 15 miles. Newark Liberty International, 16 miles. LaGuardia, 8 miles.

🛏 $$ **Excelsior Hotel,** 45 W. 81st St. (ⓒ **212/362-9200;** www.excelsiorhotelny.com). $$$ **Le Parker Meridien,** 118 W. 57th St. (ⓒ **800/543-4300** or 212/245-5000; www.parkermeridien.com).

WHY THEY'LL THANK YOU: Seeing New York as New Yorkers do.

The Big City Buzz

15

Chicago: City of the Big Shoulders

All ages • Illinois

AS A MIDWESTERN TEENAGER, CHICAGO WAS MY IDEAL OF THE BIG City: classic skyscrapers packed in a full-tilt downtown business district; a grand boulevard of luxury department stores and boutiques; immense museums stuffed to the gills with rarities and wonders; lavish restaurants and huge rambling hotels; trains rattling overhead on the El; and best of all, that silvery lake stretching to the horizon, pulling a wide vista of water and sky into the picture.

Now I'm a mom, and Chicago is still my ideal of the Big City—perhaps even more so now. Most of its major museums are absolutely kid-friendly—the **Shedd Aquarium,** the **Field Museum,** the **Museum of Science and Industry,** and the **Art Institute** ⑥⑥—and three out of the four are handily located in **Grant Park,** just east of the Loop, Chicago's primary business district. (So is the **Adler Planetarium,** 1300 S. Lake Shore Dr., which has fantabulous sky shows and exhibits on the cosmos.) There's another whole cluster of

John Hancock Observatory in Chicago.

attractions at **Navy Pier,** which thrusts out from the lakeshore just north of the Loop: It has many typical mall stores, but also the engaging **Chicago Children's Museum,** a flotilla of sightseeing boats, a small ice rink, an atrium of palm trees, and a 15-story Ferris wheel, a replica of the original built by George Ferris for the 1893 Chicago World's Fair. And we usually set aside a full day for rambling around Lincoln Park, which runs for miles along Lake Michigan and includes the **Lincoln Park Zoo,** 2200 N. Cannon Dr. at Fullerton Parkway, and the **Peggy Notebaert Nature Museum,** 2430 N. Cannon Dr., a hands-on environmental museum built into the slope of an overgrown sand dune. Just south of Lincoln Park is our favorite offbeat museum, the **International Museum of Surgical Science,** 1524 N. Lake Shore Dr., a gross-out experience that my teens lap up eagerly.

But beyond all this—and of course the obligatory excursions to **Wrigley Field** 🟢91 and the **Brookfield Zoo**—we love just walking around Chicago. The Loop is like an open-air museum of classic skyscraper architecture, where we wander with necks craned, peering upward; Michigan Avenue is my absolute favorite shopping street in the world, with its prosperous wide sidewalks and great range of stores. My daughter, of course, insists we stop at **American Girl Place,** 111 E. Chicago Ave., while the boys demand **Niketown,** 669 N. Michigan Ave. One last special place for us: the Gothic-style **Tribune Tower** at the foot of Michigan Avenue, with 138 chunks of stone from famous buildings around the world plastered into the facade at street level. I don't know why we always have to visit this spot, but it makes us happy.

So Chicago has that going for it, which is nice.

ⓘ **Tourist office,** 78 E. Washington St. (ⓒ **877/CHICAGO** or 312/744-2400; www.cityofchicago.org)

✈ O'Hare International, 15 miles

🛏 $$ **Homewood Suites,** 40 E. Grand Ave. (ⓒ **312/644-2222;** www.homewoodsuiteschicago.com). $$ **Hotel Allegro Chicago,** 171 W. Randolph St. (ⓒ **800/643-1500** or 312/236-0123; www. allegrochicago.com).

WHY THEY'LL THANK YOU: The child-friendliest Big City I know.

Boston Common
New England's Ultimate Town Green

All ages • Massachusetts

THE OLDEST PUBLIC PARK IN THE UNITED STATES, **BOSTON COMMON** (bordered by Beacon, Park, Tremont, Boylston, and Charles sts.) is a multilayered slice of history, nestled in the shadow of skyscrapers at the heart of one of America's first great cities. Standing on this sloping, tree-strewn 45-acre space, imagine what it looked like when the town fathers purchased it in 1634, when their settlement was just 4 years old and most folks needed a spot to graze their household cows and sheep. The occupying British army encamped here in the restless months leading up to the outbreak of the Revolutionary War; public gallows stood here until 1817; Martin Luther King, Jr., and Pope John Paul II both spoke here. It's Boston's living room, pulsing with the life of the city.

Many visitors confuse the rambling Common with its neighbor, the more sprucely landscaped **Public Garden,** the country's first botanical garden, where the famous swan boats glide over a man-made pond and a popular set of bronze statues commemorate the classic children's book *Make Way for Ducklings*. The Public Garden is lovely, yes, but there's something quintessentially American about Boston Common, despite the occasional bald patches of ground. It's always lively with picnickers, Frisbee and softball games, kite flyers, and busking musicians. The Frog Pond, where there really were frogs at one time, makes a pleasant spot to splash around in the summer and skate in the winter. At the Boylston Street side, the **Central Burying Ground** contains the grave of famed portraitist Gilbert Stuart; free concerts and plays are held at the bandstand. The aristocratic brick town houses of **Beacon Hill** overlook the Common along its north side, and the gold dome of the State House presides over the east end (note the eccentric codfish weather vane on top). On the Beacon Street edge of the Common, across from the State House, a stunning **memorial** designed by Augustus Saint-Gaudens honors Bostonian Col. Robert Gould Shaw and the Union Army's 54th Massachusetts Colored Regiment, the first American army unit made up of free black soldiers, celebrated in the 1989 movie *Glory*. And lest we get too historic, we should also mention the irresistibly touristy **Cheers,** 84 Beacon St. (② **617/227-9605;** www.cheersboston.com), originally the Bull & Finch Pub (a replica of the TV set is at Faneuil Hall Marketplace).

The Common is, appropriately enough, the starting point for the **Freedom Trail** (② **617/357-8300;** www.thefreedomtrail.org), a historic 3-mile walking route (follow a red line painted on the sidewalks); maps are available at the **visitor information booth** on Tremont Street. My kids enjoy its connect-the-dots approach to sightseeing every bit as much as I did as a child. A hard-core history fiend can easily spend 4 hours along the trail, but a family with restless children can easily do it in less—especially since you can quit at any point. (Just don't miss the **Paul Revere House,** at 19 North Sq., one of my childhood favorites.)

ⓘ **Greater Boston Convention & Visitors Bureau,** Two Copley Place (② **888/SEE-BOSTON;** www.bostonusa.com)

✈ Boston's Logan Airport

🛏 $$ **Doubletree Guest Suites,** 400 Soldiers Field Rd. (② **800/222-TREE** or 617/783-0090; www.doubletree.hilton.com). $ **The MidTown Hotel,** 220 Huntington Ave. (② **800/343-1177** or 617/262-1000; www.midtownhotel.com).

NEARBY: Black Heritage Trail ㊽, Boston Aquarium, Old Ironsides, Fenway Park ㉶.

WHY THEY'LL THANK YOU: Picnic and frolic in the shadow of 3½ centuries of history.

The Statue of Liberty & Ellis Island

Gateway to America

Ages 6 & up • New York, New York

THE ICON TO END ALL ICONS, NEW YORK CITY'S AWE-INSPIRING STATUE of Liberty is recognizable around the world as the symbol of American freedom. What's more, this is the city's greatest two-for-one deal: The same ferryboat takes you to the Ellis Island Immigration Museum, which turns out to be the real kid pleaser of the pair.

The Statue of Liberty (or, as she is officially known, Liberty Enlightening the World) is impressive enough from across the harbor, but close up—man, this chick is BIG. Don't be surprised if your young ones feel overwhelmed; even adults can get vertigo staring up her stately toga-clad physique. Lady Liberty weighs in at 225 tons of hammered copper, oxidized as planned to a delicate pale green, and her nose alone is 4½ feet long. Given to the United States by France, she has presided over the harbor since 1886. At present visitors cannot climb up inside the statue, but **ranger-led tours** (© **866/782-8834** or 212/269-5755) explore the promenade or go to the 10th floor observatory for fascinating historic exhibits and a peek through a glass ceiling into her ingenious steel skeleton, designed by Gustave Eiffel of Eiffel Tower fame. Even if you don't have a tour reservation, it's worth the trip to stroll around Liberty Island and gaze out over the harbor.

From the mountain of ragtag luggage stacked right inside the front doors, upstairs to the cramped dormitories and medical examination rooms (cough the wrong way and you could be sent right back to Europe), to glass cases crammed with the family heirlooms immigrants brought with them, the **Ellis Island Immigration Museum** brings history to life. Prepare to be awed by the second-floor Registry Hall, its soaring vaulted ceiling faced with

The While-Waiting-in-Line-at-Lady-Liberty Quiz

1. The Statue of Liberty weighs
   a. 225 tons.
   b. 25 tons.
   c. 225 pounds (when she's been to her step-aerobics class).

2. The statue's full official name is
   a. The Gatekeeper of Liberty.
   b. Liberty Enlightening the World.
   c. Liberty Looking for a Lost Contact Lens.

3. Sculptor Frédéric-Auguste Bartholdi is said to have modeled the statue after
   a. the Mona Lisa.
   b. Napoleon Bonaparte's girlfriend.
   c. his mommy.

4. Emma Lazarus's poem The New Colossus ("Give me your tired, your poor . . .") is engraved
   a. on the tablet Liberty cradles in her arm.
   b. on a plaque inside the base of the statue.
   c. on a tattoo on every park ranger's left bicep.

5. The engineer who designed the statue's tricky steel skeleton is also known for
   a. the Eiffel Tower in Paris.
   b. the Brooklyn Bridge.
   c. the Spaceship Earth sphere at Epcot.

6. The French intellectual who first proposed the idea for the statue was
   a. the Marquis de Lafayette.

    b. Edouard René Lefebvre de Laboulaye.

    c. Pepe Le Pew.

7. Once completed and shipped in sections to the United States, the statue almost wasn't erected because

    a. Americans lost the instructions on how to put it together.

    b. Americans hadn't raised enough money to build a pedestal for it.

    c. everybody thought it was so ugly.

8. Lady Liberty looks green because

    a. the statue's hammered-copper sheathing has oxidized as expected.

    b. pollution from New York Harbor has corroded it.

    c. she gets seasick from watching the ferries chug past all day.

9. The statue's nose is

    a. 4½ feet long.

    b. 10 feet long.

    c. 100 feet long (she could use some plastic surgery).

10. The Statue of Liberty was given to the people of the United States by the people of France

    a. because there was no room for it in Paris.

    b. in repayment of old war debts.

    c. to symbolize a special friendship between the two countries.

ANSWERS: 1. a 2. b 3. c 4. b 5. a 6. b 7. b 8. a
9. a 10. c

white tile, where new arrivals shuffled along in tediously long lines to be interviewed by immigration officials. (Cue up the theme from *The Godfather, Part II*.) On the Wall of Honor outside, some 420,000 immigrants' names are inscribed in steel. There are hands-on exhibits, films, live plays, computer stations where you can examine ship manifests—2 hours is barely enough to do this place justice.

Both sights are free, though you'll have to pay for the boat over. Ferryboats make frequent trips, running a 35-minute loop from Battery Park to Liberty Island to Ellis Island and back to Battery Park (from New Jersey you can board ferries in Liberty State Park).

ⓘ **Statue of Liberty,** Liberty Island (✆ **212/363-3200;** www.nps. gov/stli). **Ellis Island** (✆ **212/363-3200;** www.ellisisland.org). **Ferry** (✆ **212/269-5755** or 201/435-9499; www.statuecruises.com).

✈ ⊨ See Manhattan **14**.

WHY THEY'LL THANK YOU: America's beacon to the world still shines here.

---

18 American Postcards

Philadelphia: Cradle of Liberty

All ages • Pennsylvania

IT'S NO EXAGGERATION TO CALL THIS THE MOST HISTORIC SQUARE MILE in America, the very place where the Declaration of Independence was signed and the Constitution of the United States hammered out. The look is tidy and stereotypical, steepled red-brick buildings with neat white porticos. Yet there's nothing tidy about what happened here—it took enormous courage for these British colonists to leap off this cliff—and when you see your child's eyes light up, realizing that these were real people and not just Faces on the Money, that's when you'll be glad you came to Philadelphia.

The giant foot of the Statue of Liberty.

The Liberty Bell.

The focal point of Independence National Historical Park is **Independence Hall,** Chestnut Street between 5th and 6th streets, where in a chamber known as the Pennsylvania Assembly Room, the Second Continental Congress convened in May 1775. Virginian Thomas Jefferson was assigned to write a document setting forth the colonists' grievances (Jefferson worked on it while boarding at **Graff House,** nearby at 7th and Market sts.), and by July 4, 1776, the Declaration of Independence was ready to be signed by the Congress—in Independence Hall you can even see the silver inkwell they used. You can also see the Rising Sun Chair that George Washington sat in 11 years later to preside over the Constitutional

Convention, as President of the new United States. In a glass pavilion next door rests the 2,000-pound **Liberty Bell,** which was rung in 1776 at the first public reading of the Declaration; circle around it to find the famous crack up its side, which has been there since it was cast in 1751. At the northern end of grassy Independence Mall, the modern **National Constitution Center,** 525 Arch St., is so darn interactive, the children may not even notice how educational it is—you can take your own Presidential Oath of Office or try on a Supreme Court robe. In Signers Hall, bronze life-size statues depict the delegates who signed the Declaration—putting faces to those famous signatures was enormously satisfying.

A couple blocks east of the Mall, **Franklin Court,** 318 Market St. between 3rd and 4th streets, has some lively multimedia exhibits on the life and career of Philadelphia's most famous citizen, scientist/publisher/inventor/philosopher Benjamin Franklin. (You'll find more of the same out at the science museum **The Franklin Institute 57**.) But the most evocative colonial home here is the tiny **Betsy Ross House,** 239 Arch St., where a widowed Quaker seamstress supposedly sewed the first American flag. No one knows for sure if she really sewed it, or if this was even her house, but it makes a great story; and the house is so quaint, you'll want to believe it.

(i) **Visitor Center,** 6th and Market sts. (© **800/537-7676** or 215/965-7676; www.independencevisitorcenter.com)

✈ Philadelphia International

🛏 $$ **Best Western Independence Park Inn,** 235 Chestnut St. (© **800/624-2988** or 215/922-4443; www.independenceparkhotel.com). $$$ **Rittenhouse Hotel,** 210 W. Rittenhouse Sq. (© **800/635-1042** or 215/546-9000; www.rittenhousehotel.com).

WHY THEY'LL THANK YOU: Imagine John Hancock, dipping his quill pen in that inkwell.

Washington, D.C.
Having a Ball on the National Mall
All ages

WHEN CONGRESS HIRED FRENCHMAN PIERRE L'ENFANT TO DESIGN A capital city for the new United States, he came back with a supremely rational plan: a grid of numbered and lettered streets laced with diagonal avenues (named after states) and punctuated with circular plazas. In a stroke of genius, L'Enfant laid at the heart of it all the National Mall, a 2^1/$_2$-mile-long, 300-foot-wide plain lined with neoclassical government buildings—one unbroken sweep from the dome of the Capitol to the back lawn of the White House. What I wonder is this: Did L'Enfant foresee what a great place this Mall was going to be for children?

Most buildings along the Mall these days are museums, many of them run by the Smithsonian Institution, which means free admission; you can give restless kids a chance to stretch their legs between visits to the **National Museum of the American Indian** **45**, the **National Museum of Natural History,** or the **Air and Space Museum** **60**. We also love the **National Museum of American History,** Constitution Avenue NW between 12th and 14th streets, where you can see everything from the original Star Spangled Banner to gowns worn by various First Ladies, to Julia Child's kitchen and Archie Bunker's armchair. The Rotunda of the **National Archives,** Constitution Avenue between 7th and 9th streets, displays three incredibly important (and rare) original documents: the Declaration of Independence, the Constitution, and the Bill of Rights. If admission hadn't been free, we'd never have coaxed the kids into the **Freer Gallery of Art,** 1050 Independence Ave. SW, where we skipped the vast collection of Asian art just to see the amazing Peacock Room designed by James Whistler.

The National Mall.

The Mall's diversions include a 19th-century **carousel** at Jefferson Drive and the **pool** in the National Gallery's Sculpture Garden at 7th Street, where kids can splash their feet in summer and ice-skate in winter. Vendors sell ice cream and soft pretzels; families jog, bike, and fly kites. What could have been a grandiose ceremonial space becomes instead a happy picnic ground.

Visiting the **U.S. Capitol,** the Mall's eastern landmark, requires some effort; line up early at the visitor center at 1st and Independence for your timed-admission ticket for a free half-hour tour. Visiting the **White House,** at the other end, requires even more effort, beginning with a call to your congressperson 6 months in advance. But seeing the stately monuments that lie to the west requires nothing more than hopping onto a narrated **Tourmobile** tram (✆ 888/868-7707 or 202/554-5100; www.tourmobile.com) and hopping off again whenever you please. We were content to do a drive-by of Lincoln's, Washington's, and Jefferson's, but we were glad we got off for the **Vietnam Memorial** to be deeply moved by endless ranks of soldiers' names, simply etched in smooth black granite.

ⓘ **Tourist office** (✆ **202/789-7000;** www.washington.org).

✈ Ronald Reagan Washington National, 5 miles. Dulles International, 26 miles. Baltimore-Washington International, 30 miles.

🛏 $$ **Embassy Suites Hotel Downtown,** 4300 Military Rd. NW (✆ **800/EMBASSY** or 202/362-9300; www.embassysuitesdc metro.com). $$$ **Hilton Washington,** 1919 Connecticut Ave. NW (✆ **800/HILTONS** or 202/483-3000; www.washington.hilton.com).

WHY THEY'LL THANK YOU: Seeing the national treasures.

American Postcards **20**

Niagara Falls: The Big Spill

All ages • New York, USA & Ontario, Canada

Everyone's seen a Kodachrome photo of Niagara Falls, that stupendous curve of cascading water that lies between the United

Niagara Falls.

States and Canada. It's one of those sites, however, that postcards never do justice to: To stand on a viewing platform and see, really see, how big it is, to hear the thunder of falling water, to feel the mist spritzing your face is another thing altogether. This is a natural wonder kids love and should see.

There are actually two waterfalls here, both of them doozies: the American Falls and Horseshoe Falls. Both are around 175 feet high, although Horseshoe Falls, at 2,500 feet wide, is more than twice as wide as its sibling. The Canadian shore has the real panoramic view; both falls can be seen from the American side, but not together (Prospect Point for the American Falls, Terrapin Point for Horseshoe Falls). The Canadian side tends to have better hotels and more attractions. No matter where you stay, you can easily visit both, by crossing the Rainbow Bridge, preferably on foot—it's only the length of a couple city blocks. Bring a passport (or a birth certificate).

On the U.S. shore, head for **Niagara Falls State Park** (© 716/278-0337; www.niagarafallsstatepark.com) to explore the falls: An **Observation Tower** overlooks the river, and **Cave of the Winds**

(✆ 716/278-1730) takes you down by elevator onto boardwalks where you can walk around the base of the American Falls. Canada's 775-foot-high **Skylon Tower,** 52 Robinson St. (✆ 905/356-2651; www.skylontower.com), has a revolving restaurant on top, and the **Journey Behind the Falls** (✆ 905/354-1551; www.niagara parks.com) allows you to descend via elevator to tunnels punctuated with portholes that look out through the blur of water right behind Horseshoe Falls. The coolest way to see the falls, of course, is the classic *Maid of the Mist* boat ride (✆ 716/284-8897; www.maidofthemist.com), which plays no favorites; it departs from either shore. You'll chug upriver toward the American and Horseshoe Falls, sailing right up the base of both (don't worry, blue slickers are provided to keep you dry).

Want more of an adrenaline rush? Book a 10-minute helicopter ride over the cascades with **Niagara Helicopters** (✆ 905/357-5672; www.niagarahelicopters.com) or **Rainbow Air** (✆ 716/284-2800; www.rainbowairinc.com), or crash through the white waters of the Niagara gorge with **Whirlpool Jet Boat Tours** (✆ 888/438-4444 in the U.S., or 905/468-4800 in Canada; www.whirlpooljet.com). The **Great American Balloon Company,** Rainbow Boulevard South, Niagara Falls, New York (✆ 716/278-0824) offers a gentler sky-borne view.

This being a major tourist destination, there's a ton of other attractions around, from historic old forts and botanical gardens to aquariums and amusement parks. But overdeveloped as it may be, the spectacular Falls are still there.

ⓘ U.S. (✆ **877/FALLSUS** [325-5787] or 716/282-8992; www.niagara-usa.com). Canada (✆ **800/563-2557;** www.niagarafalls tourism.com).

✈ Buffalo Niagara International Airport, 34km (21 miles)

⊨ $$ **Courtyard by Marriott,** 5950 Victoria Ave., Niagara Falls, Ontario, Canada (✆ **800/771-1123** or 905/358-3083; www.nfcourt yard.com). $$$ **Red Coach Inn,** 2 Buffalo Ave., Niagara Falls, NY, USA (✆ **866/719-2070** or 716/282-1459; www.redcoach.com).

BEST TIME: May–Oct.

WHY THEY'LL THANK YOU: Roaring water, mist, and rainbows galore.

New Orleans: The Treasure We Almost Lost

All ages • Louisiana

FOR SOME PEOPLE, IT TOOK A HURRICANE FOR THEM TO REALIZE THEY should have visited New Orleans. Here was a true original among American cities, a place where people danced with parasols at funerals, ate beignets and po' boys, believed in voodoo and vampires, and threw plastic beads off parade floats. Despite its raunchy Bourbon Street reputation, it was always a great family destination. Even in the Mississippi Delta heat (and every time I've been there it was sweltering hot), something about New Orleans always seemed laid-back and incredibly cool, darlin'. And Hurricane Katrina *nearly wiped it off the face of the earth.*

Luckily, the reports of New Orleans's demise were premature—though damaged, New Orleans is still very much with us, and open again for business. You've been given a second chance. Take it *now.*

The part of New Orleans least affected by the disaster was its prime tourist area: the **French Quarter,** one of the few areas that had been built above river level and escaped heavy flooding. The French Quarter—or as local signs have it, the Vieux Carré—is, despite the name, a Spanish-flavored fantasy of wrought-iron balconies and tiny flower-filled courtyards and alluring louvered windows, its centerpiece being gardenlike Jackson Square. Just walking around here is entertainment, but several attractions are especially appealing to families: the touristy-but-fun **Historic Voodoo Museum,** 724 Dumaine St.; the kitschy **Musée Conti Wax Museum,** 917 Conti St.; the **Old U.S. Mint,** 400 Esplanade Ave., which despite the name is all about New Orleans jazz history and Mardi Gras traditions; and the open-air **French Market,** Decatur Street, from Jackson Square to Esplanade Avenue, where you can buy snacks like gator on a stick. Really.

A jazz band on Bourbon Street.

Be sure to ride the historic St. Charles Streetcar; it goes from the Quarter to the **Audubon Zoo** at 6500 Magazine St., which displays 1,800 animals among lush subtropical plantings and a replica of a Louisiana swamp (dig the white alligator). Right on the banks of the Mississippi, the **Audubon Aquarium of the Americas,** 1 Canal St., is a world-class facility with exhibits of penguins, sharks, a coral reef, a rainforest, and a swamp. And though Mardi Gras itself may be overwhelming to children, they can get an eyeful of floats and larger-than-life character sculptures at **Blaine Kern's Mardi Gras World,** 223 Newton St., Algiers Point; they can even try on some fabulous costumes.

ⓘ **Tourist office,** 2020 St. Charles Ave. (✆ **800/672-6124** or 800/748-8695; www.neworleanscvb.com)

✈ Louis Armstrong New Orleans International, 15 miles

🛏 $$ **Hotel Monteleone,** 214 Rue Royale (✆ **800/535-9595** or 504/523-3341; www.hotelmonteleone.com). $$$ **Omni Royal Orleans,** 621 St. Louis St. (✆ **800/THE-OMNI** or 504/529-5333; www.omniroyalorleans.com).

WHY THEY'LL THANK YOU: They'll know what it means to love New Orleans.

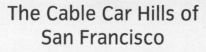

22 American Postcards

The Cable Car Hills of San Francisco

All ages • California

MAYBE IT WAS ALL THOSE RICE-A-RONI® COMMERCIALS FROM MY childhood, but I get a thrill when I hear the clang-clang of a **San Francisco cable car.** These beloved wooden icons, the only moving landmarks in the National Register of Historic Places, are absurdly impractical; San Francisco had nearly torn up all the tracks in 1947 until a public outcry saved the last three lines. And now, whaddya know, they are San Francisco's most iconic attraction, the one must-do for every visitor.

San Francisco's steep hills are notorious; it's a great location for filming car chases (remember *Bullitt?*) but a challenging place for everyone else. In 1869 engineer Andrew Hallidie watched a team of overworked horses pulling a heavy carriage up a rain-slicked San Francisco hill and resolved to invent a mechanical device to replace the beasts; in 1873 the first cable car traversed Clay Street. They really are ingenious: An electrically powered steel cable under the street constantly moves at 9½ mph, which each car clamps onto with an underground grip to get hauled along (operators are thus

A San Francisco cable car.

called "grippers," not drivers). Listen for the distinctive underground clickity-clack of the cable. Daredevils choose to ride in the open-air sections, not the enclosed seating areas, standing up and hanging onto a strap, which at under 10 mph isn't as perilous as it sounds.

Two cable car routes start at the intersection of Powell and Market streets: The **Powell-Hyde line** ends at the turnaround in a waterfront park by Ghirardelli Square, and the **Powell-Mason line** meanders through North Beach to end on the east side of Fisherman's Wharf. The Powell-Hyde line has the steepest climbs and drops, if that's what you're interested in; take it from Market Street north, past crooked Lombard Street on your right before heading down Russian Hill with a breathtaking vista of **Alcatraz** 27 and the San Francisco Bay. The **California Street line** runs east–west from Market and California streets over Nob Hill to Van Ness Avenue. Queues to board the Powell Street cars at either end seem endless, but there are strategies to avoid them: Ride at less-popular night hours, jump on at an intermediate stop (this is iffy in high season, when cars get so full that they can't pick up passengers en route), or board at Powell and Market rather than the crowded turnarounds near Fisherman's Wharf (for the California line, the Van Ness end is less crowded). Even though we waited for over an hour at the Ghiradelli Square terminus, we actually had fun—street musicians played, tourists swapped travel tips, and we could watch three or four cars pivot grandly around on the turntables. After that long wait, the ride seemed surprisingly short, but no one in my family complained.

(i) **San Francisco Municipal Railway** (© **415/701-2311;** www. sfmta.com). **Convention & Visitors' Bureau,** 900 Market St. (© **415/391-2000;** www.onlyinsanfrancisco.com).

✈ San Francisco International Airport, 13 miles. Oakland International Airport, 18 miles.

🛏 $$$ **The Argonaut,** 495 Jefferson St. (© **866/415-0704** or 415/563-0800; www.argonauthotel.com). $$ **Larkspur Hotel Union Square,** 524 Sutter St. (© **866/823-4669** or 415/421-2865; www.larkspurhotelunionsquare.com).

WHY THEY'LL THANK YOU: The San Francisco treat.

---

23 **Otherworldly Sites**

Devil's Tower
Something Strange in Wyoming
All ages • Devil's Tower, Wyoming

I KNEW MY KIDS WOULD LOVE THE SCENE IN *CLOSE ENCOUNTERS OF THE Third Kind* when Richard Dreyfuss starts sculpting Devil's Tower out of mashed potatoes. Spielberg sure picked the right natural landing pad for his alien spaceship to make contact with earthlings—there *is* something otherworldly about this stark monolith rising out of the Wyoming pines and prairies. The Northern Plains Indians called it Bears Lodge, and it has sacred meanings for them too. Even seeing a picture of it is unforgettable, but visiting Devil's Tower in person—well, that's more special than you'd imagine.

Devil's Tower.

Time for a geology lesson. Devil's Tower is what's known as an igneous intrusion, meaning that it's a column of rock hardened by molten lava that seeped long ago into a vein of sedimentary rock. A shallow sea once covered this part of the Great Plains, and most of the rock is soft sedimentary stuff like red sandstone and siltstone, with a little shale mixed in. The flat-topped cone that became Devil's Tower used to be under that sea, but once the waters had receded, centuries of erosion gradually wore away the softer rock around the igneous cone, leaving it exposed. Today the cone thrusts 1,267 feet above the surrounding pine trees and prairie grasslands. That flat top no doubt gave Spielberg the idea of an extraterrestrials' spaceport; a parachutist did land on top in 1941, drawing great publicity—especially since he then had to figure out how to get down! Vertical cracks groove the sides of the tower in almost parallel columns, giving it its distinctive furrowed look. It's well-nigh irresistible for climbers, although you must register at the visitor's center before attempting to ascend and follow strict regulations about bolts and drills. In deference to the Native American reverence for this sacred place, the park's staff urges climbers to voluntarily forego climbing in June, a month with many religious ceremonies for the local tribes.

For most of us, the best way to experience Devil's Tower is to take the 1.3-mile paved **Tower Trail** that circles around the base. It's very kid-friendly, being mostly flat (after a steep climb at the start) with benches and interpretive stations along the way. Take your time walking so that you can examine this rugged pinnacle from every angle and in different lights. Bring sketchbooks and try to draw its stern majesty. And don't be surprised if the kids start mounding their mashed potatoes at dinner that night, tracing ridges on the sides with their forks . . .

While you're here, kids shouldn't miss the **prairie dog towns** on the park's east road, where black-tailed prairie dogs scamper about, popping in and out of their subterranean condos. You came out here to see the West—well, this is about as Western as it gets.

ⓘ Off U.S. 24 (② **307/467-5283;** www.nps.gov/deto)

✈ Gillette Airport, 40 miles

🛏 See Mount Rushmore & Crazy Horse **29**.

WHY THEY'LL THANK YOU: An icon of the West with mystical power.

24   **Otherworldly Sites**

Arches National Park: Sculpted by Nature

All ages • Moab, Utah

MORE THAN 2,000 IMPOSING NATURAL STONE ARCHES PUNCTUATE THIS sandstone plateau, almost as if it were one gigantic pop-up book. These are natural formations, the result of cycles of freezing and thawing rain and snow which continually dissolve the "glue" that holds together the sand grains of the stone, chipping away at them

bit by bit over time. And yet knowing the scientific process doesn't detract from the marvel of it, a seemingly endless variety of shapes and delicate colors, as if some giant sculptor were deliberately trying to make each arch more fantastic than the one before.

It's a place to let your imagination go wild. Is Delicate Arch really so delicate, or would its other nicknames (Old Maids Bloomers or Cowboy Chaps) be more appropriate? And what about those tall spires? You might imagine they're castles, the towering masts of stone sailing ships, or the petrified skyscrapers of some ancient city. Be sure to pick up a map at the visitor center, because half the fun is matching up the formations with the fanciful names that have been given to them. On the 18-mile scenic drive from one end of the park to the other, you'll pass such features as **Park Avenue,** a solid rock "fin" that reminded somebody of the Manhattan skyline; the **La Sal Mountains,** which early explorers thought looked like piles of salt; **Courthouse Towers,** with such monoliths as Sheep Rock, the Organ, and the Three Gossips; and the **Tower of Babel.** A side road leads to the **Windows, Turret Arch,** and the **Cove of Caves,** where erosion is even now slowly making a new arch out of the largest cave. Detour onto **Wolfe Ranch Road** for a brief hike to see a 100-year-old ranch and some Ute pictographs.

Along the drive, stop to venture onto the various walking trails, many of them short and easy enough for even young children. A .3-mile walk lets you circle **Balanced Rock,** a 3,000-ton boulder perched on a slowly eroding pedestal; a .5-mile there-and-back trail leads past the **Parade of Elephants** to **Double Arch;** and another .3-mile walk goes to **Sand Dune Arch,** with an irresistible sandy hollow beneath that the kids can play in.

ⓘ U.S. 191 (℗ **435/719-2299;** www.nps.gov/arch)

✈ Grand Junction, CO, 125 miles. Salt Lake City, UT, 230 miles.

🛏 $ **Arch View Camp Park,** U.S. 191 & U.S. 313 (℗ **800/813-6622** or 435/259-7854; www.archviewresort.com). $$ **Bowen Motel,** 169 N. Main St. (℗ **800/874-5439** or 435/259-7132; www.bowenmotel.com).

WHY THEY'LL THANK YOU: Waiting for Balanced Rock to topple.

Hiking in Arches National Park.

Petrified Forest & Painted Desert
Trees of Stone, Stones of Color
All ages • Near Holbrook, Arizona

From the name, the children may expect to see standing trees of stones, leaves and branches and all. Well, a better name for the Petrified Forest might be the Petrified Pile of Logs, with its fossilized hunks of ancient trees scattered like kindling across the arid scrubby landscape. But these richly colored petrifications are plenty impressive close up, and the other half of the park, the Painted Desert, more than lives up to its name, in glowing pastel beauty.

Start at the **Rainbow Forest Museum,** the visitor center at the southern entrance to the park, where the displays will teach the kids how those petrified logs got petrified in the first place. These 225-million-year-old conifers date from the late Triassic age, when this area was an equatorial tropical forest. The trees fell, were buried in sediment, and then overlaid with volcanic ash, which gradually deposited silica in the trees that replaced their cells with quartz crystals. This unique set of circumstances left a profusion of these immense fossils in the area, which were sliced up and sold for souvenirs at such a rate that in 1906 the government stepped in to preserve what was left in this park. A short walking trail behind the visitor center winds around a hillside strewn with logs (4–5 ft. in diameter), giving the children a first chance to examine them up close; across the road a 1.5-mile loop takes you to Agate House, a ruined pueblo fashioned out of colorful petrified wood.

  Once you're back in the car, head north on the park's 27-mile scenic road. Several overlooks highlight wonders such as the **Crystal Forest** (unfortunately, tourists pried the quartz and amethyst crystals out of these logs long ago); the **Jasper Forest,** petrified trees with their roots still attached; and **Agate Bridge,** a natural bridge formed by a petrified log. In the hazy blue badlands of the

The Painted Desert.

Blue Mesa, chunks of petrified wood teeter on mounds of soft clay that are eroding away beneath them. **The Teepees** are a lovely set of hills striped with different colors. At **Newspaper Rock** you can gaze upon ancient Native American petroglyphs, with the ruined pueblos of their creators at nearby **Pueblo Parco.**

Across I-40, you'll be fully in the Painted Desert section of the park, where a series of eight overlooks let you admire the breathtaking desert colors, which were caused by various minerals in the mudstone-and-clay soil—iron, manganese, and others—which oxidized at different rates as they were exposed by erosion. It's a dreamscape of pastels washing over dramatically eroded buttes and mesas, one of nature's best special effects ever.

ⓘ U.S. 180, 20 miles east of Holbrook (✆ **928/524-6228;** www. nps.gov/pefo)

✈ Flagstaff, 90 miles. Phoenix, 180 miles.

🛏 $$$ **La Posada Hotel and Gardens,** 303 E. Second St., Winslow (✆ **928/289-4366;** www.laposada.org). $ **Wigwam Motel,** 811 W. Hopi Dr., Holbrook (✆ **928/524-3048;** www.galerie-kokopelli.com/ wigwam).

WHY THEY'LL THANK YOU: If the rock logs don't get them, the Kodachrome mesas will.

Otherworldly Sites

26

Hawaii Volcanoes National Park
Where Hot Lava Still Flows
Ages 6 & up • Volcano, Hawaii

Hawaii Volcanoes National Park beats out all the other U.S. national parks on two scores: It has the only tropical rainforest, and it has the only active volcano. Since 1983, the Big Island's Kilauea

No parking in Volcanoes National Park.

volcano has been erupting regularly, although these are "quiet" eruptions, with gas escaping slowly instead of exploding violently. Its slow-moving red lava oozes over the landscape, sometimes even over the park roads. The kids may wish they could see volcanic fireworks, but once they're here, feeling the soles of their sneakers getting gummy from the heat below, they'll realize this is spectacular enough.

This is not a tame volcano, not by any means. Over the past 2 decades, some $100 million worth of property has been destroyed by the eruptions, though the lava flow has also added 560 acres of new land. On many days, the lava flows right alongside accessible roads, and you can get as close as the heat will allow; sometimes, however, the flow is in underground tubes that spill out miles away.

Near the visitor center, you can get your first look at **Kilauea Caldera,** a 2½-mile-wide, 500-foot-deep pit with wisps of steam rising from it. Going counterclockwise on Crater Rim Road, you'll drive past the **Sulphur Banks,** which smell like rotten eggs, and the **Steam Vents,** fissures where trails of smoke, once molten lava, escape from the inner reaches of the earth. At the **Thomas A Jaggar Museum** there's a viewpoint for Halemaumau Crater, which is half a mile across but 1,000 feet deep; walk right to the rim to gape at this once-fuming old fire pit, which still gives off fierce heat from its vents. Near the Iki Crater, the .5-mile **Devastation Trail** is a sobering look at how a volcanic eruption wreaked havoc in 1959. Another intriguing stop is the **Thurston Lava Tube,** a cool underground hole in a lush forested bowl that somehow escaped the lava flow.

By now you won't be surprised to learn that the volcano goddess, Pele, was an important deity to ancient Hawaiians—you definitely wanted to be on the right side of this lady. At the 15-mile mark down Chain of Craters Road, you can see **Puu Loa,** an ancient site sacred to the Hawaiians, where a .5-mile boardwalk loop trail will show you thousands of mysterious Hawaiian petroglyphs carved in stone.

If the volcano is actively erupting, call the visitor center for directions to the best locations for night viewing—it's quite a sight, watching as the brilliant red lava snakes down the side of the mountain and pours into the cold sea, hissing and steaming ferociously. Of course, the ultimate view is from the sky: **Blue Hawaiian Helicopter** (*©* **800/745-BLUE** or 808/961-5600; www.bluehawaiian. com) runs several tours right over the bubbling caldera, for a bird's-eye view you'll never forget.

ⓘ Hawaii Belt Rd. (Hwy. 11; *©* **808/985-6000;** www.nps.gov/havo)

✈ Hilo, 30 miles

🛏 $$ **Kilauea Lodge,** 19-3948 Old Volcano Rd., off Hwy. 11 (*©* **808/ 967-7366;** www.kilauealodge.com). $ **Volcano House,** inside Hawaii Volcanoes National Park (*©* **808/967-7321;** www.volcanohouse hotel.com).

WHY THEY'LL THANK YOU: Red-hot magma.

27 Atmospheric Places

Escape to Alcatraz
America's Most Famous Prison
Ages 8 & up • San Francisco, California

WHAT DO YOU DO WITH THE MOST NOTORIOUS HARDENED CRIMINALS in the federal prison system? In 1934, at the height of the gangster era, the government had a brainstorm: Wall them up in a converted military fort on an island in San Francisco Bay surrounded by sheer cliffs, frigid waters, and treacherous currents. Just let them *try* to escape from there. Thus was the **Alcatraz Island federal penitentiary** born, a maximum-security prison whose infamous inmates included Al Capone, "Machine Gun" Kelly, and Robert Stroud (the Birdman). You may recognize its impregnable profile, lit by an ominous domed beacon tower, from such movies as *The Birdman of Alcatraz, Escape from Alcatraz,* and *The Rock;* it hasn't held a prisoner since 1963, but the vibe is still eerie—and therefore irresistible to youngsters.

The What-to-Do-While-Waiting-for-the-Ferry-to-Alcatraz Quiz

1. In what bay is Alcatraz Island located?
   a. Marin Bay
   b. San Francisco Bay
   c. The Bay Area

2. When was Alcatraz a federal maximum-security prison?
   a. 1934 to 1963
   b. 1893 to 1964
   c. 1920 to 1973

3. Which one of these people was a famous Alcatraz inmate?
   a. Mack the Knife
   b. Fred Flintstone
   c. Al Capone

4. How big was the average cell?
   a. 5 by 9 feet
   b. 10 by 12 feet
   c. 4 by 6 feet

5. How many prisoners were executed at Alcatraz?
   a. 3
   b. 0
   c. 8

6. Which three men managed to escape Alcatraz but were never seen again?
   a. The Ringling Brothers and Marshall Pickford
   b. Bobby Carson, Al Capone, and Danny Marsh
   c. Frank Morris and the Anglin Brothers

7. How many cells were there?
   a. 455
   b. 336
   c. 90

8. What was the highest number of prisoners held at Alcatraz?
   a. 325
   b. 302
   c. 208

9. How long did the average prisoner stay?
   a. Life sentence
   b. 8 years
   c. 25 years

10. What was the nickname prisoners gave Alcatraz?
   a. "The Island"
   b. "The Cage"
   c. "The Rock"

ANSWERS: 1. b 2. a 3. c 4. a 5. b 6. c 7. b 8. b
9. b 10. c

These days it's harder to get into **Alcatraz** than it is to get out of it, thanks to the popularity of National Park Service tours to the island; call at least a month in advance to reserve tickets. You'll take a ferry from Fisherman's Wharf and explore the famous prison with a slide show and audio tour, which includes fascinating stories told by former guards and inmates. As you listen to the audio narration and the grim anecdotes delivered by park rangers, you get a chilling sense of what it was like to be isolated in the middle of the bay—with winds blustering through the barred windows and armed guards pacing the gun galley—yet so achingly close to the beautiful city of San Francisco.

By declaring Alcatraz to be "inescapable," the government was almost daring prisoners to break out. Officially, no one ever did, although there were 14 audacious attempts over the years: 23 fugitives were caught, 6 were shot, 2 drowned, and 5 others were missing and presumed drowned.

The ferry ride across the bay is fun, but you'll want to wear jackets, even in summer—and wear comfortable shoes, because there are many stairs to climb. Older kids who want to ratchet up

The Rock.

the tour's already-somber tone may opt for the spooky "Alcatraz After Hours" tour. Hey, if you're going for creepy, you might as well go all the way.

(i) **Pier 33,** at Fisherman's Wharf ((C) **415/981-7625** for reservations; www.nps.gov/alcatraz)

✈ ⊨ See San Francisco Cable Cars **22**.

WHY THEY'LL THANK YOU: Appreciating the sweet taste of freedom.

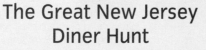

28   A Touch of Kitsch

The Great New Jersey Diner Hunt

All ages • I-95, I-80 & the Garden State Parkway, New Jersey

GLEAMING ROADSIDE RESTAURANTS OF CHROME AND BRIGHTLY COLORED enamel, where you can chow down at a Formica counter lined with swiveling stools—this is the all-American diner experience, and there's nowhere better to track it down than in highway-laced New Jersey, which has more diners than any other state in the country. Not more diners per capita, or more diners per square mile—more diners period.

Right across the Hudson River from New York City (take the Holland Tunnel), Jersey City has two classic diners worth seeking out. At the juncture of U.S. 1 and Manhattan Ave., **White Mana,** 470 Tonnele Ave. ((C) 201/963-1441), with its distinctive circular counter around the grill, was built for the 1939 World's Fair as the "diner of the future," and it does look somewhat like a red flying saucer just landed on Earth. From here, follow Route 1 to Culver Avenue and then West Side Avenue to find the neon-lit chrome-sided **Miss America Diner,** 322 W. Side Ave. ((C) 201/333-5468), built in the

New Jersey's Tick Tock Diner.

1950s. For New Jersey's oldest diner, take I-95 north to I-280 west and get off in Harrison for the red-and-white barrel-roofed **Max's Grill,** 731 Harrison Ave. (𝄐 973/483-2012). Get back on I-95 and zip north to I-80 west, where you can stop off in Hasbrouck Heights to see the 1947 **Bendix Diner,** State Road 17 and Williams Ave. (𝄐 201/288-0143), an Art Deco gem so picture-perfect that it was used not only in the 1982 film *Diner* but also the 1995 Drew Barrymore movie *Boys on the Side.* Take Route 17 farther west to Hackensack to see White Mana's sister diner, **White Manna,** 358 River St. (𝄐 201/342-0914), dating from the late 1930s, all chrome and glass blocks and hard-to-miss-from-the-road red signs. The petite burgers known as sliders are even better here than at the Jersey City location. Another classic diner a mere 20 minutes outside of Manhattan is the **Tick Tock Diner,** 281 Allwood Rd., Clifton (𝄐 973/777-0511). From New York City, take the Lincoln Tunnel to Rte 495, to Rte 3 West to reach this 1948 art deco diner that serves a mean hamburger; look for the neon clock and "Eat Heavy" sign, which are original fixtures.

Down near the Jersey Shore—Bruce Springsteen's old Asbury Park stomping grounds—are three more beauties worth a visit. The **Americana Diner** in Shrewsbury, 1160 Rte. 35 (take exit 109 from the Garden State Pkwy.; 𝄐 732/542-1658), may be a 1997 replica, but it was built by Kullman, one of the classic diner manufacturers; and it has the vintage look down pat, with lots of neon and chrome and glass-block walls. The bright and flashy **Broadway Diner** in Red Bank, 45 Monmouth St., just west of Route 35 (© 732/224-1234), is more authentic, built circa 1957, and a good breakfast stop—the pancakes here are excellent. Farther west in Freehold, the 1947 Tony's **Freehold Grille**, 59 E. Main St. (© 908/431-8607), has a particularly great period neon sign out in front and a long, sleek counter inside.

ⓘ www.njdiners.com

✈ ⊨ See Manhattan ⑭.

WHY THEY'LL THANK YOU: Landmark architecture served with a burger and a shake. You want fries with that too?

29   A Touch of Kitsch

Mount Rushmore & the Crazy Horse Memorial

All ages • Keystone & Custer, South Dakota

WHEN YOU THINK ABOUT IT, MOUNT RUSHMORE IS ONE OF THE ODDEST monuments ever: gigantic chiseled faces of four presidents. Why four? Why those four (Washington, Jefferson, Lincoln, and . . . Theodore Roosevelt?)? And why in the South Dakota badlands, miles away from most U.S. citizens? But crazy as it is, darned if another group didn't raise money to carve another mountain nearby with an even bigger sculpture, depicting American Indian chief Crazy Horse.

Mount Rushmore was the passion of one individual: Gutzon Borglum, a Danish-American sculptor from Idaho, who was hired by South Dakota to make a memorial to draw visitors to the Black Hills. Borglum—who had previously been hired to carve Stone Mountain in Georgia, until negotiations broke down—chose this peak because it was hard granite, the highest in the area, and it faced southeast, where it would catch good daytime light. He also picked which Presidents to portray: Teddy Roosevelt made the cut because he'd lived in South Dakota and was a conservationist (also because Borglum had already done a bust of TR for the U.S. Capitol). The project was conceived in 1923; sculpting began in 1927 and puttered along through the Depression. Washington was unveiled in 1934, Jefferson in 1936, Lincoln in 1937, and Roosevelt in 1939. Borglum died in 1941, and though his son Lincoln continued for 7 months, the work halted for good when the U.S. entered World War II.

Visit the **museum** under the amphitheater to learn about Borglum's innovative engineering. A 1-mile **Presidential Trail** leads to viewing terraces at the base of the mountain; take a guided tour so the kids can learn all the curious history. It's great to catch Mount Rushmore by the dawn's early light, or at least as soon as the park opens at 8am. In summer, a nightly lighting ceremony at 9pm (8pm in Sept) makes another splendid viewing op.

To many Native Americans, Mount Rushmore is a sacrilege, an intrusion on sacred landscapes, so the Lakota tribe initiated their own project 17 miles away, hiring sculptor Korczak Ziolkowski, who'd briefly worked with Borglum on Mount Rushmore. He began to hew the image of Chief Crazy Horse astride a thundering stallion in 1948; 50 years later—16 years after Ziolkowski himself had

Mount Rushmore.

died—only the chief's nine-story-high face was completed. Millions of tons of rock have been blasted from the mountain face, though, and even kids should be able to trace the form emerging from the granite; nightly laser shows in summer project the finished design onto the rough-hewn rock. When finished, Crazy Horse will be so big that all four heads on Mount Rushmore can fit inside it—641 feet long and 563 feet high. At the base of the mountain, the **Indian Museum of North America** focuses on the tribal history of numerous Native American cultures.

(i) **Mount Rushmore National Memorial,** Hwy. 244, Keystone ((C) **605/574-2523;** www.nps.gov/moru). **Crazy Horse Memorial,** U.S. 16/385, north of Custer ((C) **605/673-4681;** www.crazyhorse. org).

✈ Rapid City, 35 miles.

🛏 $$ **Alex Johnson Hotel,** 523 6th St., Rapid City ((C) **800/888-2539** or 605/342-1210; www.alexjohnson.com). $$ **Sylvan Lake Lodge,** 24572 U.S. Hwy 87, Custer ((C) **605/574-2561** or **605/574-4943;** www.custerresorts.com).

WHY THEY'LL THANK YOU: Giant statues for American giants.

30 A Touch of Kitsch

The Corn Palace: Harvest Gone Wild

All ages • Mitchell, South Dakota

ON THAT CLASSIC COAST-TO-COAST SEE-AMERICA-FIRST DRIVE IN THE family truckster, once you hit the Great Plains things begin to seem a little slow—it's just such a long way between cities. That's the appeal of the Corn Palace, sitting squarely on South Dakota's long east–west stretch of I-90. You have to get off the road somewhere, and when you do, it might as well be somewhere that makes you blink your eyes in wonder.

Turning onto Mitchell's main street downtown, you can't miss the Corn Palace, a gaudy, multicolor riot of onion domes and turrets. It was originally built in 1921 as the main exposition hall for this agricultural market town, but in a way the Corn Palace is built new every year. Every spring, a different artist announces a theme and sets to work, creating a set of **murals** to cover the outside of the Corn Palace—murals made out of *corn*. Yes, that's right, kernels and husks of real corn are applied to the facade, a custom that goes back to the 1890s when the first Corn Palace was opened. Actually, it still seems bizarre, no matter how long they've been doing it. But that's why the Corn Palace looks as though it's made out of corn, though underneath the building is mere reinforced concrete.

Concerts, stage shows, and sports events take place in and out of the hall, and still the artists work to complete their design, using thousands of bushels of native South Dakota corn, grain, and grasses. Come here in the summer and you'll still see a work in progress.

(i) 604 N. Main St. ((C) **605/996-6223;** www.cornpalace.org)

✈ Rapid City, 35 miles

🛏 $$ **Days Inn,** 1506 S. Burr ((C) **800/329-7466** or 605/996-6208; www.daysinn.com)

WHY THEY'LL THANK YOU: It's beyond corny.

A Touch of Kitsch

31

Wall Drug: The Power of Advertising

All ages • Wall, South Dakota

At the other end of South Dakota's I-90 corridor from the **Corn Palace** ㉚, Wall Drug is a one-of-a-kind phenomenon—a wayside stop that just kept growing and growing. It all began in the Depression, when nearby Mount Rushmore was still under scaffolding, years away from attracting travelers to this middle-of-nowhere burg. Desperate for business, Wall Drug's owners, Ted and Dorothy Hustead, put up signs on the highway advertising free ice water to thirsty travelers. Motorists poured in.

Now convinced of the power of advertising, the Husteads planted more and more billboards, until they even began to appear in foreign countries. The Highway Beautification Act of the 1960s severely limited Wall Drug's billboard campaign, but still the tourists came; and over the years the Husteads (who still own the place, though it's now in the hands of the third generation) have added more and more popular features to draw them in.

Some 20,000 people a day, it's estimated, pull off the road to mill around this shambling low-slung complex, so extensive that it scarcely seems like a drugstore anymore. (There is a replica of the original small pharmacy inside, however.) Along with a "mall" of 26 little shops, Wall Drug has a restaurant, a vast postcard store, a gallery selling Western art, displays of Native American artifacts, a mechanical diorama of an American Indian village, and a mocked-up main street of a Western town. But wait! There's more! Animated figures tucked into every available niche "speak" to the customers, including a roaring T-Rex. Out in the back yard stand king-size plaster figures of a bucking bronco, a rabbit, and the mythical jackalope, and an 80-foot-long green brontosaurus statue benignly casts its shade over the children's play area.

Nothing defines "tourist trap" better than Wall Drug. That's why you must visit.

ⓘ 510 Main St. (ⓒ **605/279-2175;** www.walldrug.com)

✈ ⊨ See Mount Rushmore ㉙.

WHY THEY'LL THANK YOU: Classic roadside Americana.

Winchester Mystery House
Monument to Paranoia
Ages 4 & up • San Jose, California

TRUTH CAN BE STRANGER THAN FICTION, AND NO THEME-PARK ATTRACTION could be any stranger than this actual house in San Jose, an hour's drive south of San Francisco. This quirky mansion, set in acres of meticulous gardens, was obviously the handiwork of a madwoman. Walking through it on any of the various guided tours, you'll be astonished at its weird mix of luxury, good taste, and utter craziness.

Begun in 1884, the Winchester Mystery House is the legacy of Sarah L. Winchester, a 44-year-old widow. Her husband was the son of the famous rifle manufacturer Oliver Winchester, maker of the fabulously successful Winchester repeater rifle—sometimes called the "Gun That Won the West." After both her husband and her baby daughter died, the disconsolate Mrs. Winchester consulted with a seer, who proclaimed that the family lay under a special curse—targeted by the unhappy spirits of people who had been killed with Winchester rifles. Gullible Mrs. Winchester bought the idea, and that's when her personal tragedy took a peculiar twist. The medium told her those unquiet souls could be appeased by only one thing: perpetual construction on the Winchester mansion. (Makes you wonder if she got a kickback from the contractor.) Convinced that she'd live as long as building continued, Mrs. Winchester—who happened to have a fortune to spend on this scheme—went through most of her $20-million inheritance over the next 38 years, as construction work went on 24 hours a day, 7 days a week, 365 days a year.

As you can probably guess, this is no ordinary home. With **160 rooms,** it sprawls across half a dozen acres, a red-roofed Victorian mansion with extra turrets and gables sprouting randomly. There was never any master blueprint; Sarah Winchester herself designed

Winchester Mystery House.

the additions, often drawing them on a scrap of paper or a table-cloth whenever a new idea seized her. It has some 40 bedrooms, 47 fireplaces, and 5 kitchens, and a number of high-tech features for its time—elevators, forced-air heating, and gas light fixtures that could be turned on with the press of a button. Her favorite flower was the daisy, and it's fun to look for the **daisy motif** repeated in room after room.

Still, what kids undoubtedly remember most are the many disturbing features: a staircase leading nowhere, a Tiffany window with a spider-web design, a window in the floor, and doors that open onto blank walls. Superstitious Mrs. Winchester harped on the number 13, hoping thereby to confound the vengeful spirits—there are 13 bathrooms, 13 windows and doors in the old sewing room, 13 palms lining the main driveway, 13 hooks in the séance room, and chandeliers with 13 lights. Did the perpetual renovation plan work? Well, eventually Sarah Winchester did die, but not until the ripe old age of 82—with the house still unfinished, of course.

(i) 525 S. Winchester Blvd. (I-280 at Hwy. 17; (C) **408/247-2101;** www.winchestermysteryhouse.com)

✈ San Francisco International, 45 miles

🚋 See San Francisco Cable Cars **22**.

WHY THEY'LL THANK YOU: Realizing that even grown-ups get out of control sometimes.

Carlsbad Caverns
Colossal Underground Refuge
Ages 6 & up • Carlsbad, New Mexico

NATIVE AMERICANS ALWAYS KNEW THERE WAS A GIANT CAVE SYSTEM snaking around under the porous limestone reef of the Guadalupe Mountains. But white settlers only stumbled upon it a century ago, after noticing vast hordes of bats swarming out of a hole in the ground every summer day at sunset. Some 100 caves lie within today's park, an underground world of pale limestone where every fantastic and grotesque shape imaginable (and unimaginable) has been sculpted by natural forces—from frozen waterfalls to strands of pearls, soda straws to miniature castles, draperies to ice-cream cones. Above all, what is impressive here is the sheer size of the cave, a constantly cool (56°F/13°C) refuge from the 100°F (38°C) heat outside in the Chihuahuan Desert.

The main cave open to the public, the immense Carlsbad Cavern, offers several options. With smaller kids, you may just want to take the elevator from the visitor center down 750 feet to the **Big Room,** which is a pretty understated name for this jaw-dropping rock chamber whose floor covers 14 acres. If you're more ambitious, follow the traditional explorer's route from the historic natural entrance, winding down for a mile into the depths through a series of underground rooms to the same Big Room. A self-guided tour from here runs 1¼ miles over a relatively level path, taking about an hour. Rangers along the path point out some of the more evocative formations, demonstrating the still-growing dome sta-lagmites and the daggerlike stalactites jabbing down from the ceiling.

Tours of other sections of Carlsbad Cavern range from the easy **Left Hand Tunnel,** a half-mile lantern tour, to the difficult **Hall of the White Giant** tour, which requires you to crawl long distances, squeeze through tight crevices, and climb up slippery flowstone-lined passages. The 2¹/₂-hour tour of **Slaughter Canyon Cave** is a far more strenuous cave hike from a different cave mouth alto-gether. And if the kids don't like being underground too long, they can still join one of the most popular activities at the caves, a sun-set gathering at the natural entrance (May–Oct) to watch a quarter-million Mexican free-tailed bats flap out of the cavern to wheel out over the desert for a night of insect feasting. After all, that's how the Americanos found the joint in the first place.

ⓘ 3225 National Parks Hwy. (© **877/444-6777** or 505/785-2232; www.nps.gov/cave)

✈ El Paso, 150 miles. Cavern City Airport, 23 miles.

🛏 $$ **Holiday Inn Express,** 2210 I W. Pierce (© **877/863-4780;** www.hiexpress.com)

WHY THEY'LL THANK YOU: The Big Room.

---

34 In the Wild

Arizona-Sonora Desert Museum

All ages • Tucson, Arizona

DON'T BE FOOLED BY THE NAME—THIS IS NO DUSTY INDOOR MUSEUM with dead stuffed animals, but a wide-open wildlife park with real creatures prowling around their natural settings. And the word "desert" is misleading too, for the Sonoran Desert—a huge geo-graphical area that extends from central Arizona down through northern Mexico and Baja California—contains not only arid desert lands but also forested mountains, springs, rivers, and streams. So

Arizona-Sonora Desert Museum.

while this attraction does limit itself to wildlife from the Sonoran Desert, you'll see a lot more than Gila monsters, tarantulas, and scorpions here, that's for sure.

After all, when you think *desert* you don't think *fish*—and yet there are 10,700 fish species exhibited here, from the razorback sucker to the Colorado River squawfish. You'll also see black bears and mountain lions, black-tailed prairie dogs, desert bighorn sheep, coatis, otters, beavers, gopher snakes, screech owls, and enough hummingbirds to fill an entire walk-in aviary. Endangered species that thrive here include Mexican wolves, thick-billed parrots, ocelots, and those mysterious black desert cats called jaguarundis, crouched menacingly on their stony ledges. Lizards sun themselves indolently on a rock massif just inside the entrance; coyotes and javelinas (peccaries) stalk around their compounds, surrounded by fences that are nearly invisible—you'll feel as if there's nothing between you and the animals.

Though technically the animals you see here aren't in the wild, they are in their native environment, which makes the whole thing seem less artificial. Whereas traditional zoos display a variety of exotic species, the Arizona-Sonoran Desert Museum trains its sights upon a single ecosphere, and the exhibits make a point of demonstrating the interrelation of plants and animals. Landscaping shows off a rich diversity of Sonoran plant life—a hillside of wild-flowers, a mountainside pine-oak woodland, a grassland plateau, a red rock canyon, and the most amazing cactus garden you'll ever see. About 15% of the museum is indoor exhibits (a relief on those days when the Arizona heat climbs above 100°F/38°C), notably the Earth Sciences Center, which displays a load of gems, minerals, and fossils collected throughout the region.

ⓘ 2021 N. Kinney Rd. (𝓒 **520/883-2702;** www.desertmuseum.org)

✈ Tucson, 19 miles

🛏 $$$ **Loews Ventana Canyon Resort,** 7000 N. Resort Dr. (𝓒 **800/234-5117** or 520/299-2020; www.loewshotels.com)

WHY THEY'LL THANK YOU: Expanding their concept of "desert."

35 | **In the Wild**

El Yunque: Puerto Rico's Rainforest Gem

All ages • Rio Grande, Puerto Rico

MY CHILDREN HAVE BEEN SAVING THE RAINFOREST FOR YEARS—WHAT American child hasn't been pelted with this eco-message?—but they had never actually seen one. So they willingly gave up another day at the beach in San Juan to drive west of town to the El Yunque rainforest. Within seconds of stepping through its gate, we were enveloped in a lushness so profound, we knew at once that all those school recycling projects had been worth it.

Part of the Caribbean National Forest, El Yunque is the only tropical rainforest in the U.S. National Forest system, a 28,000-acre patch of virgin forest that looks pretty much the way it did when Columbus first sighted Puerto Rico back in 1493. We spent a good hour first in the **El Portal Tropical Forest Center,** with its three pavilions setting forth the four separate forest microclimates that compose the park. The best exhibit of all, though, was simply the bridge leading to the center, set high up near the tree canopy, where we got our first close-up views of the forest's lively birds. At last we hit the walking trails through the forest, and by now we knew what to look for on our hike to the waterfalls, and what to listen for—the distinctive coqui peep of the tiny tree frogs that live here in the millions. We could spot orchids blooming in the treetops, and incredibly tall ferns swaying among the tree trunks. We hiked along the quiet signposted trail to **La Mina Falls,** which announced itself through the trees as we drew closer, not only by the roar of tumbling water but also by the unmistakable salsa beat of picnicking families with portable sound systems. On this weekend day, every family in the park, it seemed, was at the falls, sitting waist-deep in deliciously cold water on the slippery, pot-holed rock shelf below the cascades.

The other trail in the park is longer and steeper: the El Yunque trail, which winds upward through forests of sierra palm and palo colorado, before descending into the dwarf forest of Mount Britton, which is often shrouded in clouds. There are great views here from various peaks, including Yunque Rock.

The weather looked overcast when we started out, and at one point a light rain shower began to spatter upon the canopy, barely enough to get us wet. Somehow, that seemed absolutely perfect. After all, what should you expect in a rainforest if not rain?

ⓘ Rte. 191 (ⓒ **787/888-1880** from Puerto Rico; www.fs.fed.us/r8/caribbean)

✈ San Juan International, 40km (25 miles)

🛏 $$ **Comfort Inn,** Calle Clemenceau 6, San Juan (ⓒ **877/424-6423** or 787/721-0170; www.comfortinn.com). $$ **Gallery Inn at Galeria San Juan,** Calle Norzagaray 204, Old San Juan (ⓒ **787/722-1808** or 866/572-2783; www.thegalleryinn.com).

WHY THEY'LL THANK YOU: Hearing the coquis.

San Diego Zoo: Panda-monium

All ages • San Diego & Escondido, California

AS THE MOTHER OF A PANDA FANATIC, I KNEW WE HAD TO GO TO THE San Diego Zoo, one of only three zoos in the U.S. with those black-and-white **giant pandas.** But the pandas are at the far end of the park, and as we worked our way there, many other creatures diverted us from our quest, all in a lush garden environment with swooping hillsides and curving paths the children were eager to explore. By the time we finally got there, the pandas could have been an anticlimax—but they weren't. They were spectacular.

More than 4,000 creatures live here, including rare species like the **Buerger's tree kangaroos** of New Guinea, **long-billed kiwis** from New Zealand, wild **Przewalski's horses** from Mongolia, **lowland gorillas** from Africa, and **giant tortoises** from the Galápagos. Even better, we saw them in naturalistic habitats, brilliantly designed not only to make the animals comfortable but also to give zoo-goers some pretty close-up views. My favorite parts, actually, were the immense **aviaries,** where you could stand on a boardwalk and peer into a jungle canopy to spy parrots and lorikeets and other gaudy tropical birds. (My husband would vote for the **polar bears.** We had a *very hard time* getting him to leave that enclosure.)

San Diego's is a surprisingly old zoo for a West Coast institution: It was launched in 1916 by Dr. Harry Wegeforth, a shrewd zoologist who traveled around the world bartering native Southwestern animals like rattlesnakes and sea lions—a dime a dozen in California but glamorous overseas—for more exotic foreign species. He also brought back plants from every locale where animals were acquired, ensuring that their new habitations could be landscaped to feel like home. San Diego was one of the first zoos to separate animals from humans with moats instead of bars, and it has long been active in conservation efforts around the world, as well as breeding programs for endangered species. (Like the giant pandas, who had a 10-day-old new baby the day we were there.)

We were glad we invested in the value package, which allowed us to hop a ride on an express bus and take a cross-zoo trip on the cable car. But now I wish we'd had time for the two-in-one package that adds on the zoo's sister facility, the sprawling **San Diego Wild Animal Park,** 34 miles north of San Diego in Escondido at 15500 San Pasqual Valley Rd. (✆ **760/747-8702**). Here many of the animals roam freely in vast enclosures, allowing giraffes and ostriches to interact with antelopes and zebras, much as they would in Africa. Humans navigate the distances via monorail cars, walking tours, or pricey-but-unforgettable photo caravans (✆ **619/718-3000** for reservations). Grrr.

ⓘ 2920 Zoo Dr., Balboa Park (✆ **619/231-1515**; www.sandiego zoo.org)

✈ San Diego

🛏 $$$ **Catamaran Resort Hotel,** 3999 Mission Blvd. (✆ **800/422-8386** or 858/488-1081; www.catamaranresort.com). $ **Park Manor Suites,** 525 Spruce St. (✆ **800/874-2649** or 619/291-0999; www. parkmanorsuites.com).

WHY THEY'LL THANK YOU: Black and white and fun all over.

Zoos 37

Beyond Pandas at the National Zoo

All ages • Washington, D.C.

FOLKS IN WASHINGTON ARE OBSESSED WITH THE PANDAS AT THE National Zoo, and have been ever since 1972, when China gave the zoo its first pair after President Nixon's historic visit to China. It took a long time, but finally in July 2005 a giant panda cub, Tai Shan, was born at the Washington Zoo, and he's currently the biggest celebrity in the nation's capital. Well, panda schmanda—there's so much else to see up here, it'd be a shame to think it was all about the pandas.

One of the country's oldest zoos (established by Congress in 1889), the National Zoo is operated by the good folks of the Smithsonian Institution, which means that, like most Washington attractions, it's free of charge, and you can easily get here via the Metro. At 163 acres, it's not as dauntingly big as some of the other zoos in this section, but the site is a long crescent that slopes downhill from the entrance—eventually you'll have to hike back uphill again. Though it has 2,400 individual animals, they represent 400 species, the emphasis being on social groups rather than lone representatives of each species (better for breeding, for one thing). Two of the most popular exhibits are right by the entrance: the **giant pandas** and the **Cheetah Conservation Station,** where a successful breeding program has swelled the numbers of these amazingly speedy spotted cats. Strolling deeper into the zoo, I personally make a beeline for the **O-Line,** a set of cables strung above the Great Ape House for a playful pack of orangutans. I also love **Lemur Island,** where a gang of irascible-looking ring-tailed lemurs scamper around; and **Within Amazonia,** a lushly land-scaped walk-through South American rainforest, with free-ranging Goeldi's monkeys swinging on the vines, a two-toed sloth hanging motionless upside-down, and accents of color added by scarlet macaws and the intensely blue poison dart

Free-ranging monkeys at the National Zoo.

frog. A kid's farm at the far end lets younger children pet domestic animals. But on the route back, this being the National Zoo, I've got a soft spot for **Beaver Valley,** displaying such all-American icons as the beaver, the black-tailed prairie dog, and the shaggy dark American bison; a bald eagle lurks nearby, as well as the beautiful red-tailed hawk.

Other unusual specimens include a giant octopus, a wily African wildcat called the caracal, the huge-eared fennec fox, Sumatran tigers, a clouded leopard, a red panda, golden lion tamarins, kiwis and kookaburras, and the endangered Mexican gray wolf. And the **naked mole-rat,** you can't forget the naked-mole rat, one of the ugliest creatures my kids adore.

(i) 3001 Connecticut Ave. NW (© **202/633-4800;** www.si.edu/natzoo)

✈ ⊨ See the National Mall ⑲.

WHY THEY'LL THANK YOU: The cheetahs, the orangutans. And, okay, the pandas.

Zoos 38

Going Ape at the Bronx Zoo
All ages • The Bronx, New York

THE BIG KAHUNA OF NEW YORK CITY'S WILDLIFE PARKS, THE 265-ACRE Bronx Zoo is a world-class facility in every way, home to more than 4,000 animals from Siberian tigers and snow leopards to naked mole-rats and meerkats. Roaming its winding paths, it's hard to imagine that anything so urban as the Bronx is on the other side of that fence.

As befits the flagship zoo of the Wildlife Conservation Society, the Bronx Zoo accommodates most animals in extremely humane enclosures, outdoors if possible, in large environments re-creating as closely as possible the species' native habitats. This does mean that there are often long walks between exhibits, which may weary younger children. (Strollers can be rented at the entrance.) Study the zoo map as soon as you enter and plot which animals you want to visit and the simplest route to pass them. Operate on the assumption that you can't see everything in 1 day, even if your kids are good walkers. Relax, take your time, and enjoy yourselves.

From April to October, several rides help you navigate the park—an open-sided tram, the Skyfari cable car and the narrated **Bengali Express** monorail. Take advantage of the latter, which tours the Wild Asia section and shows off lots of exotic animals that can't be viewed any other way. The zoo's two star exhibits are the **Congo Gorilla Forest** and the **Butterfly Zone,** both of them fascinating—on a good day you can practically go snout-to-snout with our huge simian cousins through a wide glass window, or have immense tropical butterflies land on your outstretched hand—and **Tiger Mountain** gives you the same close-up access to the coiled power of its big striped cats. The **Children's Zoo** is surprisingly fun even for 8- or 9-year-olds, with lots of learn-by-doing exhibits (like a spider-web rope climb and a prairie dog burrow that kids can climb through).

Don't overlook the indoor exhibits, either: the deliciously creepy World of Darkness; the satisfyingly icky World of Reptiles; the chattering, capering denizens of the Monkey House; and my family's favorite, the extensive **Jungle World,** a lush, humid environment full of twittering birds and prowling cats and swinging monkeys. These make the zoo worthwhile even in winter, when many of the outdoor exhibits are closed.

ⓘ Bronx River Pkwy. and Fordham Rd. (ⓒ **718/367-1010** or 718/220-5100; www.bronxzoo.com)

✈ ⊨ See Manhattan ⑭.

WHY THEY'LL THANK YOU: Those great apes.

Miami Seaquarium
Laid-Back Dolphins in the Lagoon
All ages • Miami, Florida

Down in Florida, where it's shirt-sleeve weather year-round, you can slather on sunblock and enjoy your aquariums outdoors, with wide-open views of the real ocean just behind the exhibits. I'm not talking about the behemoth SeaWorld up in Orlando—I much prefer Miami's Seaquarium, which is more compact, is less grandiose, and doesn't gouge you for souvenirs and over-priced food every time you turn around.

Like SeaWorld, Seaquarium is big on **performing animal shows**—four theaters are the focal points of this 35-acre site; plan your visit to take in all four shows if you can. Having grown up with the TV series *Flipper* (the 1960s version, I must admit), I enjoyed the Flipper Show, which stars gray bottlenose dolphins in the very same lagoon used to film the 1990s series. The killer whale show was blessedly free of Shamu pomposity, and a pack of sea lions dove, barked, and clapped their hearts out for us in their own show. A handful of landscaped exhibits are clustered around the four theaters—you do a whole lot less hiking here than you do at Seaworld—from a pond full of flamingos to an indoor coral reef tank to a simulated mangrove forest to river shallows teeming with Nile crocodiles (oddly, not American alligators). The kids were suitably creeped out to stand surrounded by a circular channel full of swift sharks, but our favorite exhibit of all featured the **manatees**—Seaquarium is a leader in the campaign to save this endangered species.

People tend to have strong opinions about whether or not to go swimming with dolphins. If this is high on your list, reserve ahead (© **305/365-2501**) to participate in a choreographed dolphin encounter in the Flipper Lagoon, at a stiff price. Children must be at least 52 inches tall.

My daughter and I added on a trip to **Parrot Jungle Island,** 1111 Parrot Jungle Trail (© **305/400-7000;** www.parrotjungle.com), which in 2003 moved from its kitschy old coral-rock South Miami home to a new $46-million site on Watson Island, along the MacArthur Causeway near Miami Beach. Never having been to the old classic, we really enjoyed the new digs, 19 acres of protected bird sanctuary featuring trails, aviaries, a sepentarium full of reptiles and amphibians, and a boardwalk trail winding through a simulated Everglades landscape. Flying overhead are hundreds of parrots, macaws, peacocks, cockatoos, and flamingos. Continuous shows star roller-skating cockatoos, card-playing macaws, and numerous stunt-happy parrots—and you should know by now that my kids and I are suckers for that sort of thing.

ⓘ 4400 Rickenbacker Causeway (© **305/361-5705;** www.miami seaquarium.com)

✈ Miami International, 40 miles

⌷ $$ **Indian Creek Hotel,** 2727 Indian Creek Dr., Miami Beach (© **800/491-2772** or 305/531-2727; www.indiancreekhotel.com)

WHY THEY'LL THANK YOU: Flipping for Flipper.

40　　**Aquariums**

Monterey Bay Aquarium
Finding New Depths on the California Coast
All ages • Monterey, California

MY PUNSTER SON DECLARED THAT HE WANTED TO SEE A MANTA RAY IN Monterey—well, we didn't, but we saw stingrays, jaguar rays, bat rays, cownose rays, and a spider web ray, and we got almost giddy with the fun we were having. As a die-hard fan of big exhibit aquariums, I have to say this northern California stunner is probably my favorite.

Jellies at the Monterey Bay Aquarium.

Yes, it's huge, with more than 350,000 marine animals and plants on display, and it has two truly awesome big tanks you can gaze at for hours—the million-gallon **Outer Bay tank,** populated by yellowfin tuna, large green sea turtles, barracuda, sharks, giant ocean sunfish, and schools of bonito; and the three-story **Kelp Forest** with its stunning view of leopard sharks and other sea creatures lacing through the leaves of a towering kelp forest. But we all know size doesn't matter. What stirred me was how this glorious facility's displays highlight the sheer beauty of sea creatures—the feathery flutter of jellyfish, the supple grace of rays, the quicksilver flash of anchovies, sardines, and mackerel swimming in massive schools.

The site of this great aquarium was not chosen at random. It sits on the border of one of the largest underwater canyons on earth (wider and deeper than the Grand Canyon) and is surrounded by incredibly diverse marine life. One wing concentrates on the **Ocean's Edge,** exploring the kelp forest and coral reefs and other habitats of Monterey Bay—there's even a coastal aviary, reminding us that plovers and pipers and other shorebirds are part of the marine equation. **Touch pools** abound here, along with the ever-popular penguin exhibit. The other wing focuses on the deep waters of the **Outer Bay,** where the fish get bigger, more colorful, and in some cases more predatory. It seems that at any given moment, there's a naturalist somewhere in the building leading a demonstration or narrating a feeding event, and on either end of the second floor are hands-on learning areas for younger children. Between the two wings, near the entrance, a few absolutely adorable sea otters frolic in a two-story habitat.

Consider adding an excursion to Moss Landing, 25 minutes north of Monterey on Calif. 1, to take Captain Yohn Gideon's **Elkhorn Slough Safari** (© **831/633-5555;** www.elkhornslough.com), a 2-hour pontoon-boat tour of the Elkhorn Slough Wildlife Reserve. This experience is like jumping into a *National Geographic* special: Expect to see harbor seals, hundreds of waterfowl, and maybe even a raft of otters feet-up and sunning themselves.

ⓘ 886 Cannery Row (© **800/756-3737** or 831/648-4800; www.mbayaq.org)

✈ Monterey Peninsula Airport, 3 miles. San Francisco International, 100 miles.

🛏 $$ **Casa Munras Garden Hotel,** 700 Munras Ave. (© 800/222-2446 or 831/375-2411; www.hotelcasamunras.com)

WHY THEY'LL THANK YOU: Cute otters, cool sharks.

---

41 Fossils

Dinosaur Valley
In the Tracks of the Dinosaurs
All ages • Glen Rose, Texas

EVEN THE VERY YOUNGEST DINOSAUR LOVERS—AND AREN'T PRE-schoolers the biggest dinosaur fans there are?—can interpret the fossil record left in stone at Dinosaur Valley: The huge footprints in the rocks here are so unmistakable, it's easy to picture the prehistoric theropods and sauropods who made them 110 million years ago.

You'll find the prints beside the Paluxy River, a branch of the Brazos, which winds through this shady, lovely 1,500-acre park in Texas about an hour's drive southwest of Fort Worth. Late summer, when the river is low, is the best time to come. You can discern the footprints best when the rock is just slightly underwater, with the wetness darkening it. (Bring a whisk broom with you to clear any debris.) It's strikingly evident that two different types of dinosaurs walked in the moist limy mud that formed this rock. Many of the footprints (typically 15–25 in. long) show three toes and sharp claws, indicating a meat-eating dinosaur called **Acrocanthosaurus.** This guy stood 20 to 30 feet tall and walked on two legs. The even larger footprints (some more than $3\frac{1}{4}$ ft. long) were made by long-necked plant-eating dinosaurs, your basic sauropods (nicknamed **"brontosaurs"**). The kids can tell its front tracks from its back ones: The front feet were round with peglike toes, like an elephant's feet, while the back ones had large claws angling rearward. Most likely these were left by a 30- to 50-foot-long dinosaur named **Pleurocoelus.**

The tracks can easily be seen at two spots in the park: The main site is across the northwest parking lot and down some stone steps to the river; upstream is the Blue Hole, a sinkhole with many more brontosaur tracks (it's also a great place for swimming, so bring your suits). The kids will have no trouble imagining a scenario of the carnivorous Acrocanthosaurus stalking the gentle, slow-moving Pleurocoelus (originally a slab of tracks showed the meat-eater ambushing the plant-eater—to see that slab today, unfortunately, you'd need to be in New York City at the **American Museum of Natural History** 56). But what's still here is graphic evidence indeed.

The **visitor center** has replicas, foot skeletons, murals, and diagrams to help kids visualize the dinosaurs. What's more, outdoors stand two immense fiberglass models, one of a brown T-Rex and the other of a green Apatosaurus—relics of the Dinosaur World exhibit at the 1964 New York World's Fair. Built by the Sinclair Oil Company (remember the old Sinclair gas station sign with its green brontosaurus?), these models are historic artifacts in their own right. Scientists still argue over what the head of the Apatosaurus should look like, but hey, we're all still learning.

(i) (C) **254/897-4588;** www.tpwd.state.tx.us/park/dinosaur

✈ Dallas–Fort Worth International, 75 miles

🛏 $$$ **Stockyards Hotel,** 109 E. Exchange Ave., Ft. Worth
((C) **800/423-8471** or 817/625-6427; www.stockyardshotel.com)

WHY THEY'LL THANK YOU: Dinosaurs walked here.

42 Fossils

Cahokia Mounds
Metropolis of the Ancient Mississippians
Ages 6 & up • Collinsville, Illinois

IT WAS ONCE THE BIGGEST CITY NORTH OF MEXICO, WITH SOMEWHERE around 20,000 residents—farmers, hunters, craftsmen, traders, priests—at its peak in A.D. 1100–1200. Archaeologists have named them the Mississippians, but we don't know what they called themselves, since they left no writings behind. An air of mystery hangs over this site, just across the Mississippi River from St. Louis. Who were these people and what was their world like? The answers are hauntingly elusive.

Exhibits at the site's visitor center show how archaeologists play detective with the ancient past. The variety of arrowheads dug up, for example, proves that these people were sophisticated enough to trade with tribes as far away as southern Minnesota and the Gulf Coast. Experts gather that the mounds were built by hand, with workers carrying dirt in baskets on their backs from so-called "borrow pits" to the mounds. Ordinary citizens apparently lived in simple houses with pole walls and thatched roofs, but they labored to erect these immense earthen structures—109 still exist, 68 of them in this park—for public ceremonies.

After viewing the center's model of the ancient city, you can take tours of three different sections of the 2,200-acre site—

Monk's Mound.

hour-long ranger-led tours, or 30- to 45-minute self-guided walks (maps and audiotapes available) of each area. You certainly can't miss **Monk's Mound,** a four-terraced platform mound that once held the home of the city's ruler; it's the biggest mound in the western hemisphere, covering 16 acres at its base and rising 100 feet. Climb the modern steps to its now-grass-covered flat top and you gaze over a huge leveled plaza, bounded by the city's 2-mile-long log stockade wall, bits of which have been reconstructed. From this vantage point, the kids can identify several mound shapes—flat-top, conical, ridge-top—which apparently had various purposes. Unlike other cultures, the Mississippians generally did not use mounds for burials, although in a few cases skeletons have been unearthed with all the trappings of a prince or chieftain; other skeletons found are mostly those of young women or men with hands and feet cut off, which suggests they were human sacrifices. (Mound 72 was particularly full of sacrificial burials.)

Once archaeologists started to dig, they found something even more amazing: the remains of an astronomical observatory, similar to Stonehenge but built of red cedar logs instead of stones. Woodhenge, the scientists have named it. How did two prehistoric cultures on different continents each get the same idea? And why did this great Mississippian city die? Archaeologists keep on digging, for they still have a lot of questions to answer.

ⓘ 30 Ramey St. (℃ **618/346-5160;** www.cahokiamounds.com)

✈ Lambert-St. Louis International, 22 miles

🛏 $$ **Drury Inn Union Station,** 201 S. 20th St. (℃ **800/378-7946** or 314/231-3900; www.druryhotels.com). $$$ **Embassy Suites,** 11237 Lone Eagle Dr., Bridgeton (℃ **800/362-2779** or 314-739-8929; http://embassysuites1.hilton.com).

WHY THEY'LL THANK YOU: Ancient mysteries, right in America's backyard.

43 **Early Humans**

Canyon de Chelly
Hanging Out with the Anasazi
Ages 8 & up • Chinle, Arizona

FOR NEARLY 5,000 YEARS, PEOPLE HAVE MADE THEIR HOMES IN THIS spectacular pair of narrow sandstone canyons of remote northeastern Arizona. The Navajos are the most recent guardians of this land; the Ancestral Puebloans (also known as the Anasazi) left their mark too, in the giant rock amphitheaters where they created caves, dwelling rooms, and ceremonial kivas. To explore the canyons is to see centuries unfold.

Ancestral Puebloan civilization reached its zenith between A.D. 1100 and 1300, but evidence suggests that these canyons may have been occupied as early as A.D. 300. In the nooks and crannies of the canyons you'll see ancient dwellings hollowed into the rock walls and the circular sacred rooms known as kivas; the largest and most impressive ruins are the **White House Ruins** in Canyon de Chelly, which were inhabited between 1040 and 1275. You'll also see ancient tombs—the **Tomb of the Weaver** near the Antelope

House ruins, and the **Mummy Caves,** both appropriately enough in Canyon del Muerto, or the Canyon of the Dead. While most tourists simply drive along the two scenic drives—the 15-mile North Rim drive, which overlooks Canyon del Muerto, and the 16-mile South Rim drive, which overlooks Canyon de Chelly (pronounced "duh *shay*")—hire a guide and you can take the kids right down into the canyons where they can poke around these fascinating ruins. Navajo guides or local tour companies will lead you either on foot or in a four-wheel-drive vehicle. The hike down is fairly demanding, so with kids you'll probably opt to drive—there'll still be a bit of walking to reach the various ruins.

Since you'll be seeing both Navajo and Ancestral Puebloan relics, make sure the kids learn the difference between the two kinds of rock art. Dark slick streaks on the walls of the canyon walls, where water seepage reacting with iron oxide created what's known as desert varnish. Ancestral Puebloans chipped away at the desert varnish to expose the lighter-colored rock underneath in

Canyon de Chelly.

pictorial designs we now call petroglyphs. Pictographs are similar designs made later by the Navajos, using colorful paints on the sandstone walls to commemorate important tribal events. Urge the kids to take time to decipher the stories told by the rock pictures—they're windows into an ancient way of life.

ⓘ Off Rte. 191 (✆ **928/674-5500;** www.nps.gov/cach)

✈ Flagstaff, 222 miles

🛏 $$ **Holiday Inn Canyon de Chelly,** Indian Rte. 7 (✆ **888/ HOLIDAY** or 928/674-5000; www.ichotelsgroup.com). $$ **Thunderbird Lodge** (✆ **800/679-2473** or 928/674-5841; www.tbird lodge.com).

WHY THEY'LL THANK YOU: Seeing pictographs and petroglyphs.

44 **Historic Revivals**

Williamsburg, Jamestown & Yorktown
Virginia's Colonial Past
All ages • Virginia

ONE OF OUR BEST FAMILY VACATIONS EVER WAS A 3-DAY GETAWAY TO Colonial Williamsburg, one of those summer trips we'd postponed for years, waiting until all three kids were old enough to make sense of its history. The weather was sweltering hot, then pouring rain—and none of that mattered. Williamsburg works on so many levels, it's a slam-dunk. The kids learned a lot, but they also had more fun than we ever expected.

It's also a relative bargain, considering how much Williamsburg offers for the money. Rockefeller money underwrites the 301-acre site of Virginia's colonial capital, sprucely maintaining its 88 original buildings (houses, shops, offices, inns, courthouse, jail, armory, Capitol, the works) and hiring a top-notch staff to run things so graciously, 21st-century hassles seem to disappear. We bought a package pass that admitted us to three Historic Triangle sites—which we visited in chronological order: Jamestown, Williamsburg, Yorktown—as well as nearby Busch Gardens and Water Country USA. Staying on **Colonial Williamsburg** property, we could walk in and out of the historic area, and at check-in we booked as many extras as we could from a crowded activity schedule. We had dinner in one of the taverns on-site (for reservations call ✆ **800/TAVERNS**), eating surprisingly delicious authentic dishes by candlelight with live minstrels strolling around. We watched an actor channel Patrick Henry for an hour, deftly answering the audience's every question. All the costumed interpreters stationed around the site are amazingly well-informed; some of them refuse to admit they aren't living in 1770 (almost a running joke with the visitors watching them), but others are more relaxed, like the cabinetmaker who jokingly asked us to bring him some Dunkin' Donuts—and even he had PhD-level knowledge of his era, not just cabinetry but agriculture, the colonial economy, and pre-Revolutionary politics, and we were fascinated by our half-hour chat while he turned chair legs on his lathe.

Jamestown, the first permanent English settlement in the New World, was a great surprise: You can drive around the actual site, with ruins of the original buildings, but the kids got more out of the Jamestown Settlement reconstruction—they could really see the alarmingly tiny ships that brought the settlers from England in 1607, and the primitive stockaded settlement, scarcely more sophisticated than the replica Powhatan Indian village nearby. At **Yorktown,** where Washington won the final victory of the American Revolution in 1781, we drove around the battlefield route and explored a replica army camp. Next time we'll skip Busch Gardens, but **Water Country USA** was a marvelous surprise, the perfect goofy way to end our history-packed 3 days.

ⓘ **Williamsburg Visitor Center,** VA 132, south of U.S. 60 bypass (✆ **800/HISTORY** or 757/229-1000; www.colonialwilliamsburg.com)

✈ Newport News, 14 miles

🛏 $$ **Crowne Plaza Fort Magruder Hotel,** 6945 Pocahontas Trail U.S. 60 (✆ **800/496-7621** or 757/220-2250). $$ **Williamsburg**

Woodlands Hotel & Suites, 105 Visitors Center Dr. (© **800/ HISTORY** or 757/220-7960; www.colonialwilliamsburg.com).

WHY THEY'LL THANK YOU: Being extras in a history movie.

45   Historic Revivals

National Museum of the American Indian

Ages 6 & up • Washington, D.C.

AMONG THE STATELY WHITE STONE PALACES LINING THE NATIONAL MALL, this Smithsonian branch really stands out: A burnt sand-colored exterior of kasota limestone wraps around undulating walls, echoing the pueblos and hogans of the Southwest tribes; with its bands of reflective windows peering out like eagle eyes, it also reminds me of some sort of Northwest tribal totem. Inside, a huge rotunda lobby is filled with celestial references, from the equinoxes and solstices mapped on the floor to the sky visible in the oculus dome, 120 feet overhead, and nature is brought in throughout the galleries—wonderfully appropriate for a museum celebrating Native peoples.

As one of the Smithsonian's newest branches, the American Indian museum shakes off the dusty approaches of the past, and has so much more than just exhibits in glass cases. Of course, it has an amazing number of artifacts to display, with its core collection of 800,000 **Native American artifacts** assembled by George Gustav Heyer—wood and stone carvings, masks, pottery, feather bonnets, and so on, representing some 1,000 Native communities through North and South America. Children can be lost for minutes, studying some of these intricate handmade objects. While there are many fine museums showcasing one tribal group or another, this one includes all the native populations of the Western Hemisphere, and many of the exhibits are organized around cross-cultural themes. (Never before had I noticed so many connections between North and South American tribes.)

The museum's designers also purposely made this a "living" museum, with Native peoples performing, storytelling, and displaying their own art alongside the historic exhibits—and that fabulous atrium entrance turns out to be perfect for **ceremonial dances.** Workshops include **demonstrations** of traditional arts such as weaving or basket making; a roster of **films** includes a number of animated shorts that retell nature legends and creation myths. Almost every exhibit, it seems, has a video of some tribe member explaining the significance of this or that custom—a much easier way for kids to learn than reading blocks of text mounted on a wall. Again, how appropriate for a Native American museum to honor oral tradition.

Some of the exhibit themes are a bit too anthropological, or too politically complex, for children to follow, but just looking at the precious objects can be enough. A pair of traditional beaded moccasins alongside red high-top sneakers hand-painted with tribal motifs—that's the sort of thing kids intuitively get.

(i) 4th St. and Independence Ave. SW ((C) **202/633-1000;** www.nmai.si.edu)

✈ 🛏 See the National Mall **19**.

WHY THEY'LL THANK YOU: Seeing what life's like for children of the tribe.

Settling America

46

Amish Country
The Plain People of Pennsylvania
All ages • Lancaster, Pennsylvania

ROLLING HILLS, WINDING CREEKS, NEATLY CULTIVATED FARMS, COVERED bridges—Lancaster County, Pennsylvania, has a bucolic beauty that would attract visitors anyway. But most tourists come here to see the Amish, dressed in their old-fashioned black clothes and driving buggies at a slow clip-clop along country roads. Yet these folks are not actors, they are real working people, and their strict customs are meant to separate them from the modern world, not to draw attention from it. The challenge of coming here with children is to discover the essence of the Amish community without falling into the tourist trap.

Begin in quaintly named Intercourse, Pennsylvania, at the **People's Place,** 3513 Old Philadelphia Pike (✆ **800/390-8436;** closed Sun), an interpretive center that will teach kids the subtle distinctions between three local sects: the Amish, the Mennonites, and the Brethern, who settled here in the early 18th century, drawn by William Penn's promise of religious tolerance. The children will learn, for example, not to take photos of the Amish; why Amish children attend one-room schoolhouses; and why they paint hex designs on their barns. Avoiding Intercourse's gaggle of Pennsylvania-Dutch-themed shops, head west to Bird-in-Hand (another quirky name) for a 20-minute jaunt in a horse-drawn buggy at **Abe's Buggy Ride,** 2596 Old Philadelphia Pike (✆ **717/392-1794;** closed Sun)—maybe this will help youngsters appreciate the slow pace of Amish life. Stop east of Lancaster for a guided tour of the 10-room **Amish Farm and House,** 2395 Lincoln Hwy. E. (✆ **717/394-6185**). Wind up at the **Central Market** downtown (just off Penn Sq.; open Tues, Fri, Sat), the oldest farmers' market in the U.S., with its swirling fans, 1860 tiles, and hitching posts.

In summer, tourists clog the main roads around Lancaster, and horse-drawn vehicles can cause bottlenecks; get a good area map so you can venture onto quiet back roads, where you have a better chance of seeing Amish farmers in their daily rounds. Stop at local farm stands to buy their excellent produce, and you'll have a natural opportunity to exchange a few words. Perhaps the best way to get the flavor of Amish life is to stay with a farm family: The **Pennsylvania Dutch Convention & Visitors Bureau,** 501 Greenfield Rd. (✆ **800/PA-DUTCH** or 717/299-8901; www.padutchcountry. com), lists about 40 working farms that take guests. Expect simple lodgings, hall bathrooms, and filling family-style breakfasts.

ⓘ **Pennsylvania Dutch CVB,** above. **Mennonite Information Center,** 2208 Millstream Rd. (✆ **800/858-8320** or 717/299-0954).

✈ Philadelphia, 57 miles

 $$ **Country Inn of Lancaster,** 2133 Lincoln Hwy. E. (© **717/ 393-3413;** www.countryinnoflancaster.com). $$$ **Willow Valley Family Resort,** 2416 Willow St. Pike (© **800/444-1714** or 717/464-2711; www.willowvalley.com).

BEST TIME: Many Amish attractions are closed Sun.

WHY THEY'LL THANK YOU: Discovering that the Plain People are human too.

Settling America 47

California Gold Rush Country
Land of the Forty-Niners
Ages 6 & up • Hwy. 49 from Nevada City to Angels Camp, California

In a cavern, in a canyon, excavating for a mine/Lived a miner, Forty-Niner . . . Rarely do state highway numbers have historical significance, but California state highway 49 does. Winding through the hills west of Sacramento, **Highway 49** is the main road through a string of Wild West towns that had their brief but dizzying heyday in the California Gold Rush of 1849. As if frozen in time, their Main streets still have raised wooden sidewalks, buildings with double porches, saloons, and Victorian storefronts. Touring the Gold Country, the kids will feel transplanted to a movie western (hundreds of films have been shot here), to a time when the promise of an easy fortune lured thousands of adventurers to risk their all in a raw new territory. Soon enough the boom went bust—but not before it had jump-started the settlement of the whole West Coast.

It's about 100 miles along Highway 49 from Nevada City in the north to Angels Camp in the south; visiting the whole area could take several days. Here are the highlights: Start where the Gold Rush itself began—just north of Placerville in quiet, pretty **Coloma** at the **Marshall Gold Discovery State Historic Park.** Here, on the south fork of the American River, on January 24, 1848, carpenter James Marshall was building John Sutter's sawmill when he chanced upon a gold nugget. On Main Street, the largest building in town is a replica of the sawmill; exhibits at the **Gold Discovery Museum** lay out the story of the frenzy that ensued once the news got out. Notice the number of Chinese stores on Main Street, the remnants of a once-sizable community of Chinese who immigrated here to provide labor for the mines. Some 40 miles south of here, you can tour the **Sutter Gold Mine,** 13660 Hwy. 49, Sutter Creek. You'll wear a hard hat, ride on a mining shuttle, and "tag in" just like a miner. Down in the shaft, you may be able to spot gemstones and gold deposits still embedded in the quartz of the Comet Vein. The other face of the Gold Rush shows at two nearby ghost towns— **Mokelumne Hill,** nowadays one street overlooking a valley with a few old buildings, and decrepit **Volcano,** which looks almost haunted with the dark rock and blind window frames of a few backless, ivy-covered buildings. Once it had a population of 8,000; today, it's more like 100. That's what happens when a boom goes bust.

Another 30 miles farther south, Gold Rush country's most popular site, **Columbia State Historic Park,** re-creates a boom town at its lively height. Kids love roaming around its dusty car-free streets, where they can take stagecoach rides or visit a newspaper office, a blacksmith's forge, a Wells Fargo express office, or a Victorian-era saloon.

ⓘ **Marshall Gold Discovery State Historic Park** (☏ 530/622-3470; www.coloma.com/gold). **Sutter Gold Mine** (☏ 866/762-2837 or 209/736-2708; www.caverntours.com/sgmt.html). **Columbia State Historic Park** (☏ 209/536-1672; www.columbiacalifornia.com).

✈ Sacramento, 55 miles from Placerville

🛏 $$ **City Hotel,** Main St., Columbia State Park (☏ 800/532-1479 or 209/532-1479; www.cityhotel.com). $$ **Imperial Hotel,** 14202 Hwy. 49, Amador City (☏ 209/267-9172; www.imperialamador.com).

WHY THEY'LL THANK YOU: There's gold in them thar hills.

Black Heritage Trail

All ages • Boston, Massachusetts

MANY TOURISTS DON'T REALIZE THAT BOSTON HAS NOT ONE BUT TWO Freedom Trails—the Revolutionary War trail, and the Black Heritage Trail, which celebrates Boston's antislavery movement. The latter runs 1.6 miles, through Beacon Hill, the center of the free black community in the years leading up to the Civil War. Walking around this neighborhood, you get a sense of how a close-knit black community gathered, gradually developing political savvy and spreading radical new ideas. The seeds of the Emancipation Proclamation were sown here on Beacon Hill. Walking the Trail is a great way to explore an era of American history that all too often takes a back seat in Revolutionary War–obsessed New England.

The 15 marked points on the trail start at the **Robert Gould Shaw Memorial** on Beacon Street across from the State House. Shaw was the white officer who led the 54th Massachusetts Regiment, the Union's first black regiment, celebrated in the 1989 film *Glory*, and this bas-relief sculpture by Augustus St. Gaudens is incredibly affecting. Other buildings you'll pass include the homes of George Middleton, an African-American Revolutionary War soldier; successful barber John J. Smith, a free black who hosted antislavery debates both at his shop and in his home; and Lewis Heyden, a freed slave whose boardinghouse was an early Underground Railroad stop. You'll see the Baptist church where church desegregation efforts began in the 1830s (years later, after the Civil War, the same church building became Boston's first African Methodist Episcopal church).

From Memorial Day to Labor Day, National Park Service rangers lead free 2-hour **guided tours** daily along the route; the rest of the year, contact the Park Service to arrange a tour. To go at your own pace without the commentary, pick up a brochure outlining the tour at the Boston Common and State Street visitor kiosks, or from the **Museum of Afro-American History,** 46 Joy St. (℃ **617/725-0022**; www.afroammuseum.org), which is where the Trail ends. The museum's site occupies the restored **Abiel Smith School** (1834), the first American public grammar school for African-American children, and the **African Meeting House** (1806), the oldest standing black church in the United States. William Lloyd Garrison founded the New England Anti-Slavery Society in this building, where Frederick Douglass made some of his great abolitionist speeches. Once known as the "Black Faneuil Hall," it also schedules lectures, concerts, and church meetings. The museum's displays employ art, artifacts, documents, historic photographs, and other objects—including many family heirlooms. Children enjoy the interactive touch-screen displays and multimedia presentations, and the patient, enthusiastic staff helps them put the exhibits in context.

ⓘ ℃ **617/742-5415**; www.nps.gov/boaf

✈ 🛏 See Boston Common **16**.

WHY THEY'LL THANK YOU: A second Freedom Trail, just as important as the first.

49 | Black History

Dr. King's Legacy
Ages 6 & up • Atlanta, Georgia

THE CIVIL RIGHTS LEADER MARTIN LUTHER KING, JR., IS BY ANY MEASURE a great man. In his hometown of Atlanta, Georgia, the 10-block area around Auburn Avenue is one of the city's most-visited sites, encompassing King's boyhood home and the Baptist church where King, his father, and his grandfather were all ministers. While other civil rights sites may illuminate the issues of that tumultuous era better, this is the place where you'll really get a feeling for this complex, gifted man who dared to change history.

To me the real heart of the site is the historic buildings associated with King. Start out at the gracefully landscaped visitor center, where you can book tours of the sites (get here early in the day, at least in summer, because tickets do run out) and bone up on King's life and times with audiovisual programs and exhibits. First off is the **Birth Home of Martin Luther King, Jr.,** 501 Auburn Ave. (✆ **404/331-6922**), the modest Queen Anne–style house where Martin Luther King, Jr., was born on January 15, 1929, and lived until he was 12. The house has been restored to its appearance when young Martin lived here—even the linoleum is an authentic reproduction, and a good deal of King memorabilia is displayed. His father (Martin Luther King, Sr., obviously) was a Baptist minister and pastor of the **Ebenezer Baptist Church** down the street at 407 Auburn Ave. (✆ **404/688-7300**), a Gothic Revival–style church founded in 1886 and completed in 1922. Years later, from 1960 to 1968—at the height of the civil rights struggle—Martin Luther King, Jr., served as his father's co-pastor here, the two actively using their pulpit to press for social change. The National Park Service operates it as a living museum, with guided weekday tours, periodic church services, and a monthly choir performance. In nearby **Freedom Plaza** rests Dr. King's white marble crypt, surrounded by a five-tiered reflecting pool.

The district is somewhat dominated by the hulking modern **King Center,** 449 Auburn Ave. (✆ **404/526-8900;** www.thekingcenter. org), a memorial and educational center directed by King's son. It has a huge library and archives on the civil rights movement, including Dr. King's personal papers, but many visitors are most interested in the exhibition hall, where selected memorabilia of King and the civil rights movement are displayed. You can see his Bible and clerical robe and a handwritten sermon; on a grim note, there's the suit King was wearing when a deranged woman stabbed him in New York City, as well as the key to his room at the Lorraine Motel in Memphis, Tennessee, where he was assassinated. The best reason to come here is to settle down in the Screening Room to watch videos of Dr. King's most stirring sermons and speeches, including "I Have a Dream." The man's words still move us.

ⓘ **MLK, JR., National Historic Site,** 450 Auburn Ave. NE (ⓒ **404/331-6922;** www.nps.gov/malu)

✈ Atlanta

🛏 $$$ **The Georgian Terrace Hotel,** 659 Peachtree St., Atlanta (ⓒ **800/651-2316** or 404/897-1991; www.thegeorgianterrace.com). $$ **Marriott Stone Mountain Park Inn,** 1058 Robert E. Lee Dr. (ⓒ **770/469-3311;** www.marriott.com).

WHY THEY'LL THANK YOU: The "I Have a Dream" speech.

---

50 **Black History**

Alabama's Civil Rights Trail

Ages 8 & up • Montgomery, Birmingham & Selma, Alabama

WHAT SEEMS LIKE YESTERDAY'S HEADLINES TO US GROWN-UPS IS IN fact the foggy past to our kids. Take, for example, that afternoon in 1955 when a black seamstress named Rosa Parks was arrested for not yielding her seat to a white man on a Montgomery, Alabama, public bus. A controversial bus boycott (led by a young Rev. Martin Luther King, Jr.) followed, one of the first skirmishes in the civil rights battle of the 1960s. We refer to it so casually, as if everyone should know about this tumultuous era, but it's all new to the kids—and even adults may find they didn't know as much as they thought.

That 1955 street scene is re-created at the **Rosa Parks Library and Museum,** 252 Montgomery St. (ⓒ **334/241-8661;** http://montgomery.troy.edu/rosaparks/museum), with a replica of the bus Parks rode, video images, and a multimedia tableau. Wonderful interactive displays throughout the museum engage children in Parks's inspiring life as an activist. King's role, of course, was pivotal, as you'll learn on the twice-daily guided tours of the neat **Dexter Avenue King Memorial Baptist Church,** 454 Dexter Ave. (© **334/ 263-3970;** www.dexterkingmemorial.org), where King used his pulpit to press for social change. Even more evocative is the **Dexter Parsonage Museum,** 309 S. Jackson St. (© **334/261-3270;** www. dakmf.org), a simple white bungalow that's been furnished as it was in the 1950s, when King and his family lived here: You can see the study where he wrote his sermons, the dining room where activists met to plan the boycott, and a front window shattered by a bomb meant to scare King off his campaign. Downtown, the black granite **Civil Rights Memorial,** 400 Washington Ave., designed by Maya Lin, pays tribute to those who fought for racial equality.

You have to credit Alabama for embracing this anguished chapter of its past. Birmingham, 90 miles north of Montgomery, has an entire downtown district memorializing civil rights events: engrossing displays (segregated water fountains, a bombed-out bus, King's jail cell) in the **Birmingham Civil Rights Institute,** 520 16th St. N. (© **205/328-9696;** www.bcri.org); the historic **16th St. Baptist Church,** 1530 6th Ave. N. (© **205/251-9402**), where a 1963 bombing by the Ku Klux Klan killed four adolescent girls; and outdoor **Kelly Ingram Park,** where a paved Freedom Path recounts crucial events with plaques and sculptures. An hour's drive west of Montgomery in Selma, you can see the **Edmund Pettis Bridge,** site of the 1965 "Bloody Sunday" riot, where a voting-rights protest march met brutal resistance from police and local vigilantes, then stop in the **National Voting Rights Museum,** 1012 Water Ave. (© **334/418-0800**), which displays artifacts about voter-registration campaigns—just one phase of the not-yet-won war for civil rights in America.

ⓘ www.touralabama.org

✈ Birmingham, 90 miles to Montgomery

🛏 $$ **Embassy Suites Hotel Montgomery,** 300 Tallapoosa St., Montgomery (© **334/269-5055;** www.embassysuites.com)

WHY THEY'LL THANK YOU: Dr. King had a dream.

Gettysburg National Park
Blood & Sorrow in the Civil War
Ages 6 & up • Gettysburg, Pennsylvania

"AWESOME" DOESN'T BEGIN TO DO JUSTICE TO THIS VAST BATTLEGROUND, where thousands of Union and Confederate soldiers clashed for 3 sultry July days in 1863. As Abraham Lincoln himself said in his famous 1864 speech here, this land has been consecrated by blood—over 50,000 deaths—and an almost-eerie atmosphere hangs over this tranquil patch of rolling farmland, now peppered with war monuments.

The park visitor center has an excellent light-and-sound presentation with a scale-model map of the battlefield, which is quite helpful—after all, the battle raged over a large patch of country in the course of 4 days, and there's a lot to keep straight. Audiotapes are available for self-guided driving tours around the 250-acre battle site, but we found that this was one place where it paid to invest in a personal guide, who drove us in our station wagon around the battlefield for 2 hours. Gettysburg's guides are gold mines of Civil War information, tailoring the tour to your particular interests; there wasn't a question we lobbed at him that he couldn't handle, whether biographies of the commanders or the physics of cannon fusillades.

We were completely engrossed by **Seminary Ridge,** where the main Confederate forces were camped; we could look down the hillside where the heroes of Pickett's Last Charge plunged to their gallant end. But we were most moved by **Little Round Top,** where a plucky band of Northern soldiers held the high ground against a furious Confederate onslaught surging up out of the boulder-strewn hollow called Devil's Den. Observation towers near Seminary Ridge give you a great aerial overview, but walking around the landscape is the only way to appreciate how hard-won every inch of ground was.

The **Cyclorama Center,** next to the visitor center, a 360-degree depiction of Pickett's Charge painted in 1883, is just the sort of pre-video-era special effect I love. In the town of Gettysburg itself, we enjoyed the **American Civil War Museum,** 297 Steinwehr Ave. (✆ **717/334-6245**), which tells the full Civil War history in waxwork dioramas; normally I find wax figures hokey or creepy but this was actually tasteful and informative. The most special part of our visit, though, was seeing the costumed reenactors—many of them amateur Civil War buffs here for the fun of it—socializing around campfires or demonstrating their rifle skills. For a flicker of a moment we traveled through time, feeling the Gettysburg tragedy in our bones.

ⓘ **Visitor Center,** 1195 Baltimore Pike (✆ **717/334-1124,** ext. 8023; www.nps.gov/gett)

✈ Baltimore-Washington International, 60 miles

🛏 $$$ **Holiday Inn Battlefield,** 516 Baltimore St. (✆ **717/334-6211;** www.ichotelsgroup.com). $$ **Quality Inn,** 380 Steinwehr Ave. (✆ **800/228-5151** or 717/334-1103; www.gettysburgqualityinn.com).

WHY THEY'LL THANK YOU: Brother fought brother on this bloody ground.

Battlegrounds 52

Remembering the Alamo
Ages 4 & up • San Antonio, Texas

Visiting San Antonio without going to the Alamo is like visiting London and not seeing Big Ben: You can do it, but it would be wrong.

Expect the kids to be let down at first. The Alamo looks downright dinky, set smack in the heart of downtown San Antonio, surrounded by skyscrapers and traffic. But the whole point of the Alamo is that it *was* such a tiny fort, and the valiant Texan volunteers never had a ghost of a chance of escaping the siege—and still they fought, they fought to the death. That's heroism, Texas style.

There were only 188 Texans defending the Alamo in February 1836, facing the 4,000-strong army of General Santa Anna, who was bent on squashing the Texas territory's bid for independence from the new Mexican Republic. The Texans held out doggedly for 13 days, waiting for reinforcements that never arrived, until all the men—every last one of them, including pioneer heroes Davy Crockett and Jim Bowie—were killed in a crushing dawn attack on March 6. But a month later, when Sam Houston was leading another troop of Texans into the battle of San Jacinto, he fired them up with the cry, "Remember the Alamo!" With that heroic example to live up to, the Texans fought like demons, and this time they won, becoming the independent Republic of Texas. (It didn't join the U.S. until 1846.)

What you see today isn't much of a fort—in 1836 the fortified compound was a bit larger, its outer walls ringing much of what is today Alamo Plaza (look for foundation stones near the steps down to River Walk). After the defeat at San Jacinto, the retreating Mexican forces pulled down much of the Alamo fort so that the Texans couldn't easily refortify it. Only two original buildings remain. First is the gabled stone **mission church**—now officially a Shrine, so show respect by removing hats and taking no photos—which was built in 1756 for the Mission San Antonio de Valero, founded in 1718 to convert local Native American tribes. By the end of the 18th century, the mission had been secularized and turned over to a Spanish cavalry unit, which renamed it the Alamo (Spanish for "cottonwood") after their Mexican hometown. Besides the church, you can visit the **Long Barracks,** originally the missionaries' living quarters, or *convento,* and later a barracks for the cavalry troops. A **museum of Texas history,** with in-depth exhibits on the battle, is in the barracks, but the children will be more affected by **artifacts** displayed in the church: things like a Bowie knife, Crockett's buckskin jacket, and one of the antiquated flintlock rifles the Texans used to defend the fort. Several cannons from the battle are set around the courtyard, mute witnesses to that day of incredible valor.

(i) 300 Alamo Plaza ((C) **210/225-1391;** www.thealamo.org)

✈ San Antonio International, 8 miles

🛏 $$ **Crockett Hotel,** 320 Bonham St. ((C) **800/292-1050** or 210/225-6500; www.crocketthotel.com)

WHY THEY'LL THANK YOU: Heroes against the odds.

O Say, Can You See

The Ships of Baltimore's Inner Harbor

All ages • Baltimore, Maryland

PAST THE SEAWALL, JUST BEYOND THE HUGE DOMINO SUGAR SIGN, you can see cargo ships and active naval vessels docked in Baltimore Harbor, still a working deep-water port. But the **Inner Harbor** is the place where visitors cluster, thanks to redevelopment that loaded the old waterfront with the Harborplace shopping mall, the **National Aquarium,** and a host of other tourist venues (a Hard Rock Cafe, an ESPN Zone, you know the drill). The Inner Harbor development somehow got it right: It's compact but not crowded, and the authentic seaport feeling is kept alive by a collection of vintage seagoing vessels, which our kids clambered around happily for an afternoon. Add a Baltimore Orioles game at Camden Yard, within walking distance, and we had a weekend that made everyone in our family happy as clams.

Our favorite ship was the **USS *Constellation,*** a triple-masted sloop-of-war launched in 1854. The *Constellation* is the last Civil War–era vessel still afloat, and it was the first ship moored here. My kids eagerly prowled her gun decks, visited the wardrooms, watched a cannon being fired, and learned about the life of a sailor from the costumed staff member on board; when it came time for the hourly raising-of-the-colors ceremony, they put on costumes and tugged the flag cords like seasoned salts.

The Harbor's other three ships, packaged as the Baltimore Maritime Museum, are also fascinating, if newer. It doesn't take much time to scoot around the gray iron decks of the Coast Guard Cutter *Taney,* the last floating survivor of the bombing of Pearl Harbor, which also was involved in the battle of Okinawa. Plunging into the underwater bowels of the **submarine USS *Torsk*** tested my sons' claustrophobia, but it's not every day you get to see inside a ship that torpedoed the last Japanese warships in World War II. The sturdy lightship *Chesapeake*—you can't miss that bright-red hull with CHESAPEAKE in huge white letters—also saw war duty (it was painted a quiet gray during the war), but spent most of its days as a floating lighthouse riding the rough waters at the mouth of Chesapeake Bay. Past the Aquarium, we also climbed up the Seven-Foot Knoll Lighthouse to see the gigantic **Fresnel light.**

In the War of 1812, this prime harbor was a prize the British navy wanted badly—but star-shaped **Fort McHenry,** East Fort Avenue (✆ **410/962-4290;** www.nps.gov/fomc), across the water, protected Baltimore from British attack in 1814, in the battle Francis Scott Key commemorated in the "Star Spangled Banner." We rode the water taxi over to the fort, where we sprawled on the slopes and tried to picture the battle. We could almost see the rocket's red glare illuminating the Inner Harbor before us.

ⓘ Piers 3 and 5, Inner Harbor (✆ **410/396-3453;** www.balto maritimemuseum.org)

✈ Baltimore-Washington International

🛏 $$$ **Baltimore Marriott Waterfront Hotel,** 700 Aliceanna St., Inner Harbor East (✆ **410/385-3000;** www.baltimoremarriott waterfront.com). $$ **Brookshire Suites,** 120 E. Lombard St. (✆ **410/ 625-1300;** www.harbormagic.com).

WHY THEY'LL THANK YOU: Playing hide-and-seek between decks.

---

54 History at Sea

Mystic Seaport
Salty Thrill of a Vintage Shipyard
Ages 6 & up • Mystic, Connecticut

ONCE A DYNAMIC WHALING AND SHIPBUILDING CENTER, THE TOWN OF MYS-tic, Connecticut, is the perfect place for an open-air village that's all about maritime life. The heart of its collection is an ever-growing cache of some 500 ships, 2 centuries' worth of seagoing vessels, powered by everything from oars and sails to steam paddle wheels and engines. Standing on the Seaport's **re-created waterfront,** we gazed out across the wide estuary of the Mystic River and found it just about impossible not to feel the lure of the open sea.

Rather than adhering to one historic period, Mystic Seaport adheres to its nautical theme. Yes, there are the requisite print ship, cooperage, schoolhouse, general store, and tavern, but the 17-acre site also features a ropewalk, a boat shed, a sail loft, a rigging loft, a lifesaving station, even shops for ship carvers and makers of nautical instruments. Staff members working in these shops aren't dressed in costumes and they aren't actors; they are real experts in the crafts they demonstrate, and delighted to share their knowledge with visitors—and somehow this makes the site feel more authentic, not less.

The most important ships in the collection have been designated national landmarks: the three-masted square-rigged whaler **Charles W. Morgan** (1841); the 1866 sloop smack **Emma C. Berry,** a graceful wood-hulled fishing boat; the 1908 paddle-wheeled excursion

Mystic Seaport.

steamer **Sabino;** and the 1921 two-masted fishing schooner **L. A. Dunton.** But the one that my kids found most fascinating to climb aboard was the replica of the impossibly cramped slave trade schooner **Amistad,** which was re-created right here in the Seaport's restoration workshops. Museum buildings on-site display extensive collections of things like scrimshaw and ship models and figureheads. A variety of boat trips are offered; inquire at the desk when you arrive, because once you've wandered around the site for a while, the urge to get out on the water becomes pretty strong. When you exit for the day, ask the gatekeeper to validate your ticket so you can come back the next day for free.

ⓘ 75 Greenmanville Ave. (Rte. 27; ℂ **888/973-2767** or 860/572-5315; www.mysticseaport.org)

✈ Providence, 45 miles

🛏 $$ **Hilton Mystic,** 20 Coogan Blvd. (ℂ **800/445-8667** or 860/572-0731; www.hiltonmystic.com)

WHY THEY'LL THANK YOU: Going down to the sea in ships.

---

55 World War II

Day of Infamy: Pearl Harbor

Ages 8 & up • Honolulu, Hawaii

TODAY HAWAII IS SO SYNONYMOUS WITH LEIS, LUAUS, AND TROPICAL suntans, it's weird to realize that most Americans had barely heard of this South Pacific U.S. possession before December 7, 1941, when the horrifying news came over the radio: Japanese bombers had attacked U.S. ships at Pearl Harbor, Honolulu. Hawaii wasn't even a state, but it was still American soil, which was under attack for the first time since the War of 1812. President Franklin D. Roosevelt called it "a day that will live in infamy," and after years of pretending that World War II wasn't our fight, we realized it was. Pearl Harbor is a site that inspires reflection on war and peace and our place in the global community.

The **USS *Arizona* Memorial** at Pearl Harbor is a truly special monument. Just 6 feet below the surface of the sea, you can see the deck of the 608-foot battleship USS *Arizona*, which sank in a swift 9 minutes, killing 1,177 of its men, more than half the total casualties that tragic day. Oil still oozes up from its engine room to stain the harbor's calm blue water—some say the ship's still weeping for its lost crew. Moored a short distance from shore, the memorial is a stark white rectangle with a scooped-out roof that spans the hull of the ruined ship; on its walkways you can ponder over the ship's bell, dredged up from the wreckage, and a shrine room with the inscribed names of the dead. The gallant flagpole overhead is attached to the mainmast of the sunken ship. You'll ride out to the memorial on Navy launches from the visitor center; go early if you can, because you'll wait 2 to 3 hours at midday. A 20-minute film and exhibits at the center fill in the history for the kids while you're waiting for your assigned ship time.

Two other ships in the harbor tell the rest of the World War II story, so you're not left on a tragic note. Next to the *Arizona*, you can board a World War II submarine, the **USS *Bowfin*** (© 808/423-1341; www.bowfin.org), nicknamed the "Pearl Harbor Avenger" for the way it harried the Japanese throughout the rest of the war. This is a great place to see how submariners lived in their cramped underwater quarters. From the *Bowfin*'s visitor center you can also visit the **USS *Missouri*** (© 877/MIGHTYMO; www.ussmissouri.com), a 58,000-ton battleship that fought at Tokyo, Iwo Jima, and Okinawa. Fittingly, the Japanese surrender was signed on September 2, 1945, on the deck of the *Missouri*. The guided tour, complete with 1940s music played on the shuttles to the ship, is a fascinating look at a massive seagoing vessel.

ⓘ Pearl Harbor (© **808/422-0561;** www.nps.gov/usar)

✈ Honolulu International

🛏 $ **Hawaiiana Hotel,** 260 Beach Walk (© **800/367-5122** or 808/923-3811; www.hawaiianahotelatwaikiki.com). $$$ **Outrigger Waikiki on the Beach,** 2335 Kalakaua Ave. (© **800/OUTRIGGER** or 808/923-0711; www.outrigger.com).

WHY THEY'LL THANK YOU: Staring through the waves at a watery grave.

American Museum of Natural History

Discovering Dinosaurs

All ages • New York, New York

HOW MANY CHILDREN HAVE FALLEN IN LOVE WITH DINOSAURS IN THE echoing galleries of this world-class New York City museum? And the dinosaurs are only the tip of the iceberg: Over the years, Holden Caulfield brooded over its collection of Northwest Indian totem poles in *The Catcher in the Rye;* in the planetarium, Woody Allen wooed Diane Keaton in the 1979 film *Manhattan;* and curious scientists plonked Daryl Hannah's mermaid into a tank to examine her in the 1984 movie *Splash.* It's one of America's great museums, and invariably engrossing for children.

When you enter the magnificent rotunda at the top of the Central Park West steps—named for Theodore Roosevelt, the outdoors-loving President who helped found the museum—a rearing skeleton of a mommy dinosaur protecting her baby from a small, fierce predator clues you in that the dazzling interactive fourth-floor dinosaur halls are the perennial star attraction. But our favorite sights are the superb dioramas in the **North American Mammals**—the grizzly bear raking open a freshly caught salmon, majestic elks lifting their massive antlers, wolves loping through eerie nighttime snow—or, on the floor above, the bi-level **African Mammals Hall,** where you can circle around a lumbering herd of perfectly preserved elephants or check out the giraffes browsing by their water hole. In the dimly lit **Ocean Life** room, a gargantuan model of a blue whale swims overhead while dolphins arc through plastic waves. Around the corner, the less-well-visited **North American Forest** dioramas are our family secret—a peaceful part of the museum where you can hunt for blue jays in oak trees and rattlesnakes behind the cactus. Haunting music playing in the **African**

and **Asian peoples** sections lull you into studying precisely detailed displays of cultural artifacts: a Chinese bride's ornate sedan chair, a pygmy's blow darts, a re-creation of a Siberian shaman healing rite, a Yoruba ceremonial costume made of red snail shells.

The stunning **Rose Center for Earth and Space,** a 95-foot-high glass cube, includes an interactive exhibit on the nature of the universe, where you can step on a scale that shows your weight on Saturn, see an eerie phosphorescent model of the expanding universe, and touch cosmic debris. There are an IMAX theater, a space show, and always at least a couple of traveling exhibitions (my only quibble with the museum is the substantial extra fees charged for these, on top of an already hefty admission price). But there's enough to do here that you don't need to go for the extras. Wander at will, keeping your eyes open and your imagination at the ready. It's a magical place.

ⓘ Central Park West and 79th St. (℅ **212/769-5100;** www.amnh.org)

✈ ⛏ See Manhattan ⑭.

WHY THEY'LL THANK YOU: The dioramas and the dinosaurs.

---

57 **Science Museums**

Franklin Institute
In the Spirit of Old Ben Himself
Ages 4 & up • Philadelphia, Pennsylvania

LET'S NEVER FORGET THAT BENJAMIN FRANKLIN WAS A SCIENTIST AS well as a statesman, publisher, and philosopher: The Franklin stove and bifocal glasses were just two contraptions he invented, and of course there's that whole experiment with the kite in the thunderstorm. It warms my heart to visit the Franklin Institute in Philadelphia,

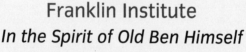

The Hall of African Mammals at the AMNH.

which pays homage to the quirkiest of our Founding Fathers. At the core of this museum is the **Franklin National Memorial,** with a 30-ton statue of its namesake and an evocative hands-on gallery on Franklin's inventions and the scientists he inspired. While it looks all stately and neoclassical on the outside, however, this place wouldn't reflect the spirit of Franklin if it didn't have a fascinating clutter of other exhibits that simply encourage kids to putter around.

Hands-on is the watchword at the Franklin Institute; pick up a schedule of the museum staff's frequent **daily demonstrations** so you won't miss the fun stuff. The collection of science- and technology-oriented exhibits ranges from a gigantic walk-through heart to the Train Factory, where you can play engineer for a 350-ton locomotive, to a Van de Graaff generator that'll make your hair stand on end at the Electricity gallery. Kid Science, on the lower level, uses a dramatic animé-like storyline to teach basic science concepts to children ages 5 to 8. On the third floor, Sir Isaac's Loft demonstrates the principles of Newtonian physics with Rube Goldberg–ian machines, noisemakers, and light shows. The Sports Challenge section was intriguing, looking at the science behind popular sports like surfing and rock climbing, and we couldn't resist the Skybike, which you can ride along a 1-inch cable three stories above the atrium floor. The whole museum is all about curiosity, and it's one of the best embodiments of the scientific method you'll ever play in.

In the warmer months, a great **high-tech playground** sprouts out on the lawn, where young kids can really mess around with science concepts—the step-on organ is a crowd pleaser, as are the maze and the high-wire tandem bicycle. If your kids like this kind of stuff, you'll probably also want to devote some time to the nearby **Please Touch Museum,** 210 N. 21st St. (© **215/963-0667;** www. pleasetouchmuseum.org).

ⓘ Logan Circle, 20th St. and Benjamin Franklin Pkwy. (© **215/448-1200;** www.fi.edu)

✈ ⊨ See Philadelphia **18**.

WHY THEY'LL THANK YOU: Playing with electricity at Ben Franklin's museum.

The Exploratorium
The Ultimate Hands-On Museum
All ages • San Francisco, California

"THE BEST SCIENCE MUSEUM IN THE WORLD" IS WHAT *SCIENTIFIC American* magazine once called this San Francisco attraction, right by the waterfront parks of the Marina District. Set in a sprawling former airplane hangar, every bit of floor space is taken up with inventive activity stations and displays that just cry out for young-sters to press, jiggle, squeeze, fiddle, poke, and manipulate to their heart's content. I've been there with toddlers and I've been there with teens, and everyone has always been totally absorbed. They don't seem to care that they're also learning scientific concepts, in a way that will really stick.

The Exploratorium staff is constantly engaged in dreaming up new exhibits, so there's no guarantee that the stuff we loved won't have been replaced by something even cooler by the time you get there. The giant soap-bubble maker is perennially popular, as is the shadow wall, the visual distortion room, and machines that make sand patterns with sound waves. The **Tactile Dome** is an amazing experience for older kids, where they grope their way around in complete darkness, dependent on senses other than sight. Across Marina Boulevard, at the end of the Marina breakwater, you'll find one of the Exploratorium's most intriguing inventions: the **Wave Organ,** a hunk of concrete embedded with listening tubes that lead underwater to translate the ebb and flow of ocean currents into strange gurgles and humming sounds.

There's a handmade quality to many of the displays that I find very appealing—clearly they've been bolted and knocked together out of plywood, wires, PVC pipes, whatever is on hand, and I can't help but think this encourages kids to become putterers and inventors themselves. As my kids get older, their interests change; the last time we were there, they gravitated to exhibits on principles of light,

117

optics, and perception, whereas in years past they were engrossed in the simple physics concepts demonstrated in the section on matter. Biology and electricity sections on the mezzanine are fascinating too. (There's a **play area** for under-4s, a godsend if you need to entertain a toddler while your older kid works the exhibits.) On our most recent visit, I watched my continually squabbling son and daughter sit for 15 minutes on either side of a mirrored pane of glass, watching their grinning faces blend together as lighting levels were gradually raised and lowered—so much for hating your siblings.

You'll find local youngsters here, not just tourists and bored school groups. It's a noisy, high-raftered, under-lit space and eventually we hit overload and have to bail out. But we never leave because we've run out of things to do.

(i) 3601 Lyon St. ((c) **415/397-5673**; www.exploratorium.org)
✈ ⨿ See San Francisco Cable Cars ㉒.
WHY THEY'LL THANK YOU: Hands-on = brains on.

Flight History **59**

Kitty Hawk
The Wright Brothers Learn to Fly
Ages 4 & up • Kill Devil Hills, North Carolina

THE NAME KITTY HAWK IS FOREVER ASSOCIATED WITH ORVILLE AND Wilbur Wright—it says so right on North Carolina's license plates. That's the place where, on December 17, 1903, this brother-brother team from Dayton, Ohio, achieved the world's first sustained, controlled, heavier-than-air powered flight. (You need all those adjectives to distinguish the Wrights' flight from a mere glider or hot-air balloon flight.) But you could score big trivia points for knowing that the Wrights didn't take off from the town of Kitty Hawk, but from a nearby 90-foot-high dune called **Kill Devil Hill** on the Outer Banks, a bony finger of land that separates the Atlantic

Ocean from the inner sounds and estuaries of North Carolina's coast. Ask the kids: If you were flying an experimental aircraft into the teeth of gusting Atlantic winds, would you really want to launch from a place called Kill Devil Hill?

Desperate to get home to Dayton in time for Christmas, Orville and Wilbur did get the Wright Flyer off the ground that windy December day in 1903, keeping it aloft for 59 seconds and flying a distance of 852 feet. Their feat is commemorated at the **Wright Brothers National Memorial,** an imposing 60-foot-high pylon of white North Carolina granite, erected in 1932 on Kill Devil Hill. In fact, the Wrights made four successful flights that day, of increasing lengths; numbered markers on the long slopes show how far they made it each time, until on the fourth go the Wright Flyer crash-landed. The visitor center features a replica of that **Wright Flyer,** plus a glider they flew here in 1902, along with a few exhibits telling the Wright Brothers' story; park rangers lead twice-daily tours, present talks at the visitor center, and run afternoon family activities such as kite flying or paper-airplane building. You can explore reconstructions of the hangar Orville and Wilbur built for their plane and their workshop/living quarters. The main thing, though, is to stand on the big grassy dune and feel the breezes rise off the water; it suddenly becomes clear why the Wright brothers traveled all the way to North Carolina to get their spidery winged craft aloft.

Not far away, at the highest sand dune on the East Coast, 138-foot-high Jockey's Ridge, you can try out those Outer Banks winds yourself by taking a hang-gliding lesson from the world's largest hang-gliding school, **Kitty Hawk Kites,** near the visitor center of Jockey's Ridge State Park (milepost 12 off U.S. 158 Bypass; ✆ **252/441-7132**). Beginning, intermediate, and advanced instruction are provided; for reservations, call ✆ **877/359-8447** or 252/441-4127; or go to www.kittyhawk.com.

ⓘ Milepost 8, U.S. 158 Bypass (✆ **252/441-7430;** www.nps.gov/wrbr)

✈ Norfolk International, 81 miles

🛏 $$$ **The Tranquil House Inn,** 405 Queen Elizabeth St., Manteo (✆ **252/473-1404;** www.tranquilinn.com). $$ **Cahoons Cottages,**

7213 S. Virginia Dare Trail, Nags Head (✆ **252/441-5358**; www.cahoonscottages.com).

WHY THEY'LL THANK YOU: Feeling the wind beneath their wings.

Flight History **60**

National Air and Space Museum
Plane Fantastic
All ages • Washington, D.C.

THE ONE DO-NOT-MISS STOP FOR FAMILIES VISITING OUR NATION'S capital, Air and Space is pretty much the star player on the Smithsonian museum team, at least as far as kids are concerned. I still catch my breath when I walk into its sleek entrance hall off the Mall and see all those **historic aircrafts** dangling from the ceiling—the Wright brothers' historic 1903 Wright Flyer, Charles Lindbergh's *Spirit of St. Louis*, the *Enola Gay* bomber that devastated Hiroshima, the *Friendship 7* capsule that took John Glenn into space. Jaded as I am by IMAX movies, I made a point of having my kids sit through the classic *To Fly*, still my favorite of the genre; we spent another afternoon out in Virginia at the satellite location so we could see the space shuttle *Enterprise*. Whether you come here for the history, the science, or just the technothrill of seeing so much heavy metal, Air and Space delivers the goods.

Air and Space holds the largest collection of historic aircraft and spacecraft in the world; only about 10% of what it owns is actually on display, even with the annex out in Virginia. Besides gawking at the famous planes hanging out in the lobby, kids love to walk through the **Skylab orbital workshop;** other galleries highlight the solar system, U.S. manned spaceflights, and aviation during both world wars. You can sneak in some hard science education with **How Things Fly,** an interactive exhibit that demonstrates principles of flight and aerodynamics (the wind and smoke tunnels are especially fun), and get into some heady astrophysics with

Explore the Universe, which probes theories about how the universe took shape. But this big, noisy, kid-packed museum isn't the sort of place where you want to be serious and thoughtful; besides the IMAX movie we wanted to do all the pumped-up extras like the **flight simulators** and the **space show** at the planetarium—admission to the museum is free, but very few families get away without buying a ticket for one of these add-ons.

The second part of the museum is out near Dulles Airport in Chantilly, Virginia, at 14390 Air and Space Museum Pkwy., where two gigantic hangars—one for aviation artifacts, the other for space artifacts—accompany a 164-foot-tall **observation tower** for watching planes land and take off at Dulles. The **space hangar** is the length of three football fields—it has to be in order to house such huge artifacts as the space shuttle, rocket boosters, spacewalk capsules, and a full-scale prototype of the Mars Pathfinder lander. The scale of this technology is awesome, and you just can't appreciate it unless you stand right next to these babies and crane your neck upward.

ⓘ Independence Ave., between 4th and 7th sts., SW (✆ **202/633-1000;** www.nasm.si.edu)

✈ ⊨ See the National Mall **19**.

WHY THEY'LL THANK YOU: Historic flying machines soaring in the lobby.

61 **Flight History**

Kennedy Space Center: 10 . . . 9 . . . 8 . . .

Ages 4 & up • Titusville, Florida

SPACEFLIGHT HAS LOST SO MUCH OF ITS GLAMOUR THAT IT CAN BE HARD for kids to comprehend how exciting it once was to watch a mighty booster rocket blast off from the launchpad at Cape Canaveral. So pop in a DVD of *The Right Stuff* or *Apollo 13* before your trip to the

Space Coast. Make them see how being an astronaut was once the coolest job a kid could aspire to.

You don't have to be a space buff to be awed by the sheer grandeur of the facilities at NASA's primary space-launch facility. Begin your visit at the **Kennedy Space Center Visitor Complex**—though it's a bit theme-park-slick, it does outline the history of space exploration well, and there are real NASA rockets on display, as well as (the coolest thing to me) the actual Mercury Mission Control Room from the 1960s. Hands-on activities, a daily "Encounter" with an astronaut, and an IMAX theater make this a place where kids will want to hang out. The **Astronaut Hall of Fame,** a separate attraction at the center, pays tribute to the Mercury, Gemini, and Apollo space jockeys, along with even more vintage spacecraft—a Mercury 7 capsule, a Gemini training capsule, and an Apollo 14 command module—and several space-y simulator rides. Plan ahead (call ✆ 321/449-4400 for a reservation) to snag a **lunch with an astronaut**—even such greats as John Glenn, Jim Lovell, Walt Cunningham, and Jon McBride have taken their turns in this daily event.

Narrated **bus tours** depart every 10 minutes to explore the sprawling space-center grounds. Stops include the LC-39 Observation Gantry, with a dramatic 360-degree view over launchpads; the International Space Station Center, where scientists and engineers prepare additions to the space station now in orbit; and the Apollo/Saturn V Center, which includes artifacts (a moon rock to touch!), films, interactive exhibits, and the 363-foot-tall Saturn V, the most powerful U.S. rocket ever launched. It's not all Disney-fied, which in my opinion is a plus, but if the kids get restless (especially given the typical Florida heat), you can hop on the next bus and move on.

The real thrill, of course, is to see a **shuttle launch;** call ✆ 321/867-5000 or check www.ksc.nasa.gov for a schedule of upcoming takeoffs (always an iffy thing, depending on weather or equipment problems), then buy tickets at the visitor complex or online at www.ksctickets.com. Or view shuttle launches the way the locals do: from the causeways leading to the islands and on U.S. 1 as it skirts the waterfront in Titusville.

Kennedy Space Center.

ⓘ NASA Pkwy. (Fla. 405; ℂ **321/449-4444** for info, 321/449-4400 for reservations; www.kennedyspacecenter.com)

✈ Melbourne International, 22 miles. Orlando International, 35 miles.

⇌ $$$ **DoubleTree Hotel Cocoa Beach Oceanfront,** 2080 N. Atlantic Ave., Cocoa Beach (ℂ **800/552-3224** or 321/783-9222; www.cocoabeachdoubletree.com). $$ **Riverview Hotel,** 103 Flagler Ave., New Smyrna Beach (ℂ **800/945-7416** or 386/428-5858; www.riverviewhotel.com).

WHY THEY'LL THANK YOU: Huge rockets up close.

Inventions 62

Hoover Dam
Concrete Colossus of the Southwest
Ages 6 & up • Boulder City, Nevada

U.S. 93, WHICH RUNS BETWEEN LAS VEGAS, NEVADA, AND KINGMAN, Arizona, lays its ribbon of concrete right across one of the great engineering wonders of the world, Hoover Dam. Built between 1931 and 1935, this behemoth Depression-era project redrew the map of America: If it hadn't been for Hoover Dam, Arizona and California would never have had enough electricity and water to sustain their subsequent population boom. And yes, the dam also created the largest artificial lake in the United States, 110-mile-long **Lake Mead.** Driving across Hoover Dam, traffic crawls as motorists gape at the view, with smooth Lake Mead on one hand and a plummeting gorge on the other. But why let the kids be content with a mere view, when you can go inside the belly of the beast?

Going face to face with this much concrete is an awesome experience. Hoover Dam stands 726 feet tall from bedrock to the roadway atop it. At the top, it's 45 feet thick, which is stout enough, but it widens the farther down you go, until at the base it's a whopping 660 feet thick. The dam was named after Herbert Hoover, not just because he was president when the bill was signed to build it, but because the Boulder Canyon dam was in many ways his idea—as Secretary of Commerce in the early 1920s, Hoover, a civil engineer himself, first urged the southwestern states to consider such an undertaking.

While much of the Hoover Dam story is told via **historic photographs** in interpretive galleries, the part kids really remember is taking **elevators** 500 feet down into the wall of Black Canyon, then walking down a 250-foot-long tunnel to look at the guts of the power plant, with its eight huge generators. At the end of the tour, don't miss going up to the observation deck to get that **panoramic view** of Lake Mead and the Colorado basin. Functional as it is in many ways, the dam still has a streamlined Art Deco flair—check out the sculptured panels decorating the central two elevator towers rising from the top of the dam, the Nevada one celebrating the dam's benefits—flood control, navigation, irrigation, water supply, and power—the Arizona one paying tribute to Indian tribes that once lived here.

Hoover Dam makes a handy day trip from Las Vegas, 30 miles away, though I'd recommend combining a Hoover Dam visit with a stay on Lake Mead in a **houseboat** (contact **Seven Crown Resorts,** Box 16247, Irvine, CA; ✆ **800/752-9669;** www.sevencrown.com). Another fun way to visit the dam is on a **paddle-wheeler cruise** from **Lake Mead Cruises** (✆ **702/293-6180;** www.lakemead cruises.com).

ⓘ U.S. 93 (✆ **866/730-9097** or 702/494-2517; www.usbr.gov/lc/ hooverdam)

✈ ⊨ See Las Vegas ⑬.

WHY THEY'LL THANK YOU: Feeling the power of those generators.

Griffith Observatory
Planetarium Hollywood
Ages 6 & up • Los Angeles, California

FILM BUFFS INSTANTLY RECOGNIZE THIS STREAMLINED ART DECO **observatory** in L.A.'s rambling Griffith Park from the climactic scenes of the 1955 James Dean classic film *Rebel Without a Cause*. My kids, however, know it from the climactic scenes of the 1999 Steve Martin–Eddie Murphy comedy *Bowfinger*. But so what if they don't get the *Rebel Without a Cause* reference? Who could fail to dig this white stucco complex with its three bronze domes, slung into the south side of Mount Hollywood with a killer panorama of Los Angeles spread out below? In the daytime, the lawn of the observatory is one of the best places in the city to view the famous Hollywood sign; on warm nights, with the lights twinkling below, the Griffith Observatory's wide terrace is one of the most romantic places in L.A. And if you manage to steer the children inside to do a little stargazing while you're up there at night, you're ahead of the game.

This Hollywood Hills landmark was built in 1935 in the vaguely Mediterranean style studio moguls of that era favored, and underwent a major renovation during 2003–06. A white obelisk in front honors six great astronomers of the past: Hipparchus, Copernicus, Galileo, Kepler, Newton, and Herschel. The large central dome houses a state-of-the-art **planetarium,** where narrated projectors display the stars and planets that are nearly impossible to observe outdoors, what with all the smog and light pollution of the L.A. metrosprawl. Like most planetariums, it also screens various multimedia shows of varying scientific seriousness. We generally skip the planetarium, however, and head straight into the adjacent **Hall of Science,** which holds exhibits on galaxies, meteorites, and other astronomical subjects—cool objects like a mechanical orrery, a Tesla coil, and scales where you can check your weight on different

The L.A. skyline from the Griffith Observatory.

planets. A Foucault pendulum mesmerized my boys as it methodically swung in the main rotunda, demonstrating the earth's rotation, and detailed 6-foot topographical models of the earth and the moon provide focal points in the side galleries.

The observatory's two flanking domes each house a telescope—in the west one, a triple-beamed **solar telescope** trained on the sun for daytime visitors, in the east one a 12-inch **refracting telescope.** On clear nights visitors can climb to the roof and wait their turn to gaze through it at the moon and planets. This is, after all, an observatory, and although it has never had the astronomical prestige of its California neighbor **Mount Palomar,** it does attend to sky matters.

ⓘ 2800 E. Observatory Rd., Griffith Park (✆ **213/473-0800;** www. griffithobs.org)

✈ Los Angeles International

🛏 **$$ Beverly Garland's Holiday Inn,** 4222 Vineland Ave., North Hollywood (🕾 **800/BEVERLY** or 818/980-8000; www.beverly garland.com). **$$ Roosevelt Hotel, Hollywood,** 7000 Hollywood Blvd. (🕾 **800/950-7667** or 323/466-7000; www.hollywoodroosevelt. com).

WHY THEY'LL THANK YOU: A chance to study the other Hollywood stars.

Stargazing **64**

Mauna Kea
Stargazing at the Top of the World
Ages 13 & up (summit), 10 & up (visitor center) • Mauna Kea, Hawaii

THE SNOWCAPPED SUMMIT OF MAUNA KEA—THE WORLD'S TALLEST mountain, if measured from its base on the ocean floor—is the best place on earth for astronomical observation. It's not just the height, it's also its location near the equator, where clear, pollution-free skies give way to pitch-black nights undisturbed by urban light. That's why Mauna Kea is home to no fewer than 13 world-class telescopes, including the **Keck Telescope,** the world's largest. Even with the naked eye, the stargazing from here is fantastic.

Many tours that go to the summit won't take anyone under 16 or any pregnant women, due to the high altitude. If you opt not to go up, it's still cool to view the model of the Keck Telescope down in Waimea, 65-1120 Mamalahoa Hwy. (🕾 **808/885-7887;** www.keck observatory.org). Developed by the University of California and the California Institute of Technology, the Keck is an infrared telescope eight stories high, weighing 150 tons, and with a 33-foot-diameter mirror made of 36 perfectly attuned hexagon mirrors—like a fly's eye—rather than one conventional lens.

You'll need a four-wheel-drive vehicle if you do drive up the mountain. **The Onizuka Visitor Center,** named after a Hawaiian

The view from the summit of Mauna Kea.

astronaut who died in the *Challenger* explosion, is an hour's drive from Hilo or Waimea; from Highway 190, take the narrow, rutted Saddle Road (Hwy. 200) 28 miles, then turn onto unmarked Summit Road and go another 6¹/₄ miles to the visitor center. At this point you're already 9,000 feet up, so stop for half an hour to acclimate. With younger kids, this may be your endpoint, so time your visit to join the nighttime **stargazing sessions,** 6 to 10pm, which include a lecture, a video, and the chance to peer through 11-inch, 14-inch, and 16-inch telescopes.

It's 6 miles from here to the summit, but it can take 45 minutes to drive this rough, unpaved, winding road, in low gear all the way—a climb of another 4,200 feet—to 13,796-foot-high **Observatory Hill.** Dress warmly and drink lots of liquid; wear dark glasses to avoid snow blindness, and use plenty of sunscreen. At the top, 11 nations, including the U.S., Japan, the U.K., France, and Australia, have set up 13 powerful infrared telescopes to look into deep space. On this bare peak, their bulbous pale domes sprout around a loop of road like alien spacecraft plopped down on the moon. Visitors can't use those telescopes, of course, though you can look at a couple (including the Keck) from galleries. (They won't be active until night, anyway.) If you take a narrow footpath past the observatories, however, there's a cairn of rocks where you can sit and contemplate an incredible 360-degree view across the Pacific. Even if you're socked in by clouds, it's a true top-of-the-world view, with the summits of Mauna Loa and Maui's Haleakala poking through the puffy white cumulus clouds beneath your feet.

(i) (C) **808/961-2180;** www.ifa.hawaii.edu/info/vis

✈ ⊨ See Hawaii Volcanoes National Park ㉖.

WHY THEY'LL THANK YOU: That monster telescope, that killer view.

Masterpieces of Art

65

The Metropolitan Museum of Art
Manhattan's Treasure Trove
All ages • New York, New York

THE ECHOING MARBLE-CLAD GREAT HALL TELLS YOU AS YOU ENTER that this is a Serious Art Museum. But don't let that put you off— New York City's number-one tourist attraction can be a lot of fun for children, even toddlers. Make a beeline for the areas kids really love: **Arms & Armor** (first floor), the extensive **Egyptian rooms** (also on the first floor—don't miss the glorious mummies), **musical instruments** (second floor, off the American Wing's courtyard), the **Costume Institute** (ground floor—rotating installations will often be of interest to kids), and the **European and American furniture rooms** (all over the place—any kid who's read *From the Mixed-Up Files of Mrs. Basil E. Frankweiler,* about a brother and sister who hide out for weeks in the Met, will adore these). On the first floor of the American Wing, a side gallery displays vintage baseball cards, and a whole gallery of grandfather clocks ticks away on the second floor. Older kids who are beginning to appreciate art may go for the **impressionist gallery** (second floor), full of Monets and Van Goghs they'll instantly recognize, or the **Lehman**

Pavilion, set up like the town house of a wealthy collector—it's art in small enough doses that it doesn't overwhelm.

Our favorite corner, hands down, is the **courtyard of the American Wing,** a light-filled open space with plantings, benches, and statues kids can actually relate to (a mountain lion and her cubs, a pensive Indian brave). Back in the corner is an entire Frank Lloyd room, all dark wood and low-slung right angles, that our family could move into at a moment's notice. Bring lots of small change for kids to throw into the American Wing reflecting pool and in the pool in front of the Egyptian Wing's serene **Temple of Dendur.** In the Japanese galleries, find the room overlooking the Temple of Dendur; off the musical instruments gallery, find the balcony overlooking the mounted knights in armor. Be sure to check out the new, airy Greek and Roman art wing. Get the idea? Wander around this immense museum, keep your eyes open, and be willing to walk away from anything that doesn't interest your children.

The huge museum gift shop has a lot of good stuff for kids, and there are plenty of free children's programs.

(i) 1000 Fifth Ave. ((C) **212/535-7710;** www.metmuseum.org)
✈ ⊨ See Manhattan **14**.
WHY THEY'LL THANK YOU: Great art is great art.

The Art Institute of Chicago
Hitting Art's Highlights in the Loop
Ages 4 & up • Chicago, Illinois

MY KIDS ARE GREAT FANS OF THE MOVIE *FERRIS BUELLER'S DAY OFF,* the greatest Chicago travelogue ever made, in my opinion. What Ferris (Matthew Broderick) and his two pals do in Chicago while playing hooky from their nice North Shore high school is our dream itinerary for a day in the Windy City: a Cubs game, a parade—and a stroll through the Art Institute of Chicago. If it was fun enough for Ferris, my kids figured, it would be fun enough for them.

Of course we were compelled to begin, like Ferris, with the immense pointillist canvas by George Seurat, **Sunday Afternoon on the Island of La Grande Jatte.** Like every other visitor there, we alternated standing up close to see the individual dots, then standing way back until the dots blur into a busy panorama of springtime in the park. But like the Seurat painting, The Art Institute has so many individual pieces of art, you can lose the big picture. The trick is to steer them to see the things they'd love before they hit Museum Overdose. After *La Grande Jatte,* we wandered dreamily through the rest of the **impressionists,** a collection so rich in Renoirs and Monets that we almost felt a sugar high; we hunted down the Van Gogh self-portrait and then Picasso's blue-period *The Old Guitarist* and felt very satisfied.

Going from the hazy impressionists to sharply detailed 20th-century American paintings was a bracing contrast. We homed in on two masterpieces: the iconic **American Gothic** by Grant Wood, which they've seen spoofed so often, and Edward Hopper's evocative late-night diner scene **Nighthawks.** Then off we went to my favorite nook in the museum: the reconstructed turn-of-the-century **Chicago Stock Exchange trading room,** a dazzling Louis Sullivan showpiece with art-glass insets and stenciled decorations and molded plaster capitals—a perfect expression of Gilded Age tycoonery.

From there, we zigzagged back to the **Thorne Miniature Rooms,** filled with tiny reproductions of furnished interiors from European and American history (heaven for my dollhouse-loving daughter) and then rewarded the boys for their patience with a browse through the great hall of **European arms and armor,** where more than 1,500 objects range from horse armor to maces to poleaxes.

We missed the world-famous collection of glass paperweights; we missed the splendid Japanese wood block prints—who cared? We didn't even worry about plotting a logical course through the museum, since scuttling back and forth allowed us to pass Marc Chagall's jewel-toned **stained-glass windows** more than once, always a good thing.

ⓘ 111 S. Michigan Ave. (✆ **312/443-3600;** www.artic.edu)

✈ ⍇ See Chicago ❿.

WHY THEY'LL THANK YOU: Connecting the dots.

Huntington Library
Pasadena's Great Portrait Gallery
Ages 6 & up • San Marino, California

THE WORD "LIBRARY" IN THE NAME MAY MAKE THE KIDS WINCE——WHY visit a musty old library on vacation? Well, even if they wanted to, they couldn't flip through the rare items in Henry E. Huntington's book collection. What they can see, though, is his terrific **art collection** in a stately Italianate mansion on a 207-acre hilltop estate.

As a girl, I was captivated by one pair of paintings here: Thomas Gainsborough's **The Blue Boy** and Thomas Lawrence's **Pinkie,** a long-haired boy in blue satin and a slim, dark-haired girl in a filmy white gown and pink bonnet, warily eyeing each other from facing walls of a wood-paneled salon. These life-size paintings capture the moodiness of adolescence so perfectly, you almost expect the kids to step out of those frames and start dissing each other. Blue Boy—aka Jonathan Buttall, son of a wealthy hardware merchant—peers guardedly at us, left hand cockily set on his hip. My sons thought his lace-collared outfit was "kinda sissy"; I explained that it wasn't the style of his time, but an homage to Flemish painter Anthony Van Dyck. Pinkie—in real life Sarah Barrett Moulton, an aunt to the Victorian poet Elizabeth Barrett Browning—stands poised on tiptoe, the satin ribbons of her askew bonnet fluttering, one hand raised defensively. Stormy skies boil behind both subjects, mirroring their defiant teenage expressions. *Pinkie* was painted 25 years after *Blue Boy,* and there was no specific connection between the two—until Henry Huntington bought them both and set them here, a sort of blind date for eternity.

It's always interesting to see great art in a private home setting (if nothing else, it's less intimidating for children than a big formal Art Museum), but it's particularly apt for 18th-century English portraits, which were originally commissioned by aristocrats to decorate their own country manors. The Huntington's main gallery presents the best assemblage anywhere of **full-figure English portraits,**

with work by Romney and Reynolds as well as Gainsborough and Lawrence—the Fab Four of late-18th-century portraiture. And the Huntington adds the final touch by serving daily **high tea** (or at any rate what Americans think of as high tea, with pastries and finger sandwiches) in a tearoom overlooking a fabulous rose garden (call ☎ **626/683-8131** for reservations, at least 2 weeks in advance). For locals, the **botanical gardens** are the Huntington's main draw—an exotic cactus garden, a lush jungle garden, soothing lily ponds, and a Japanese garden with open-air house, koi-filled stream, and Zen garden. The gardens are lovely indeed, but *Blue Boy* and *Pinkie* are what make us return.

ⓘ 1151 Oxford Rd. (☎ **626/405-2100** or 800/838-3006; www. huntington.org)

✈ ⊨ See Griffith Observatory **63**.

WHY THEY'LL THANK YOU: Blue Boy and Pinkie, sitting in a tree . . .

68 Music

The Nashville Music Scene
Country Music's Capital
Ages 8 & up • Nashville, Tennessee

NASHVILLE: THE VERY NAME IS SYNONYMOUS WITH MUSIC, SPECIFICALLY the brand of country music played on the Grand Ole Opry radio show, broadcast from here since 1927. To perform on the Grand Ole Opry is to officially "make it" in country music, and thus it's a town buzzing with music-biz execs, state-of-the-art studios, and happening clubs, with a surprising amount of jazz and rock going down as well. I love Nashville, and even though I'm no country-music aficionado, it only takes a couple hours here to get hooked on its twangy energy.

The Blue Boy, a modern interpretation.

A music pilgrimage to Nashville centers on three areas: downtown near Ryman auditorium, the original home of the Opry; in the West End along 16th Avenue, known as Music Row, where you can often spot music stars going in and out of the studios; and east of town at the vast Opryland complex where the Opry relocated in 1974. Out at Opryland, the current **Grand Ole Opry House**, 2802 Opryland Dr. (© **615/889-6611;** www.opry.com), produces three live TV shows a week, April to December—order your tickets well in advance. Exhibits at the **Grand Ole Opry Museum** next door at 2804 Opryland Dr. celebrate Opry stars past and present. For a more rounded idea of country music, though, head downtown for the **Country Music Hall of Fame and Museum,** 222 5th Ave. (© **800/852-6437** or 615/416-2001; www.countrymusichalloffame.com). From sequin-spangled costumes to historic guitars to over-the-top custom cars (a crucial status symbol in country music culture), it's an impressive roundup of artifacts, and the kids really get into the video and audio clips, interactive jukeboxes, and touch-screen computer kiosks, exploring the differences between intertwined musical genres—bluegrass, cowboy music, rockabilly, Cajun, honky-tonk, country swing. Once you're grounded in the music, walk 2 blocks to the **Ryman Auditorium,** 116 5th Ave. N. (© **615/889-3060;** www.ryman.com), aka the Mother Church of Country Music (built as a church in 1892, it still has stained-glass windows). Dowdy as it looks outside, inside it's a finely restored arena-like theater with top acoustics. By day, it offers memorabilia exhibits, a backstage dressing room tour, and a booth where you can record your own live CD; by night, it has a full roster of live concerts. Then take in an early-evening show at the **Bluebird Café,** 4104 Hillsboro Rd. (© **615/383-1461;** www.bluebirdcafe.com), to hear today's up-and-coming singer-songwriters.

ⓘ **Nashville Visitor Information Center,** Gaylord Entertainment Center, 501 Broadway (© **615/259-4747;** www.visitmusic city.com)

✈ Nashville International, 8 miles

🛏 $$ **Courtyard Marriott Nashville Vanderbilt/West End,** 1901 W. End Ave. (© **800/245-1959** or 615/327-9900; www. marriott.com). $$-$$$ **Opryland Hotel,** 2800 Opryland Dr. (© **615/458-2800;** www.gaylordhotels.com).

WHY THEY'LL THANK YOU: When their boots start a-tapping.

Rock 'n' Roll Hall of Fame: Cleveland Rocks

Ages 6 & up • Ohio

WHY CLEVELAND? WHY NOT? THIS IS THE TOWN WHERE DJ ALAN FREED first coined the term *rock 'n' roll,* where Chuck Berry played his first public gig; it's the hometown of musicians from Phil Ochs to Chrissie Hynde to Trent Reznor. And what's more, it's within a day's drive of 50% of the U.S. population, so this high-profile shrine can be visited by as many music lovers as possible.

Designed by I. M. Pei, the museum building is an all-shook-up mass of porcelain-tiled geometric shapes, piled up like a guitar and amps in the back of a roadie's van, with a glass pyramid jutting out from one side over Lake Erie. Inside is a cool collection of **pop-culture memorabilia** to browse through. Even if you and the kids don't listen to the same artists, there's plenty here for everyone to groove on. Exhibits display programs, posters, photos, instruments (from Junior Walker's lovingly shined saxophone to a smashed guitar from Paul Simonton of the Clash), and stage costumes (James Brown's red rhinestone-studded tuxedo coat, Neil Young's fringed leather jacket). But what really grabs kids are the artifacts from rock stars' childhoods—things like Jimi Hendrix's baby picture, Jim Morrison's Cub Scout uniform, John Lennon's report card, Joe Walsh's high-school football jersey. Not to ignore current chart toppers, on the plaza level a rotating exhibit features today's artists. For those of us who actually remember the 1950s, the **Rave On exhibit** displays mementos from rock 'n' rollers like Eddie Cochran, Buddy Holly, and the Everly Brothers on a curved wall evoking a chrome-and-neon diner.

Still, rock 'n' roll isn't about artifacts, it's about performance, which is why it's stirring to watch the filmed Hendrix performance in the **Jimi Hendrix Surround Sound Theater.** Up in the **Hall of Fame,** a video collage of all the 200-plus inductees is mesmerizing. The

Hall of Fame includes mostly musicians (eligible 25 years after their first record release), as well as a few producers, DJs, and journalists. Though displays near the entrance focus on the most recent class of inductees, huge "virtual jukebox" stations let you access just about any song recorded by any Hall of Famer; their autographs are etched in glass on a great wall projecting over the lake. As with all such ventures, the list of who's in and who's not is controversial, but then that makes for great dinner-table arguments.

(i) (©) **888/764-ROCK** or 216/781-7625; www.rockhall.com

✈ Cleveland International, 10 miles

🛏 $$ **Cleveland Marriott Downtown,** 127 Public Sq. ((©) **800/ 228-9290** or 216/696-9200; www.marriott.com). $$ **Holiday Inn-City Center Lakeside,** 1111 Lakeside Ave. ((©) **888/465-4329** or 216/241-5100; www.ichotelsgroup.com).

WHY THEY'LL THANK YOU: It's only rock 'n' roll, but they'll like it.

The Movies **70**

Hooray for Hollywood: Movie Mecca
Ages 8 & up • Hollywood, California

THE NAME HOLLYWOOD MAY BE SYNONYMOUS WITH MOVIEMAKING, but many tourists are disappointed by how shabby the town itself is. I relish its seedy, down-at-heels aura, but my kids were not impressed—until they got an eyeful of **Grauman's Chinese Theatre,** 6925 Hollywood Blvd. ((©) **323/463-9576**), still one of the world's great movie palaces, with over-the-top Chinese embellishments and an entry court where stars like Elizabeth Taylor have set their signatures and hand- and footprints in cement. So what if the kids didn't recognize most of the names? Nearby is the recently built **Kodak Theatre,** 6834 Hollywood Blvd., where they give out the Oscars every year; we also marveled at the refurbished

Egyptian Theatre, 6712 Hollywood Blvd., and the Art Deco **Pantages Theatre,** 6233 Hollywood Blvd., for a *Sunset Boulevard* taste of 1920s glamour. Stars who couldn't get a spot at Grauman's were honored with bronze medallions in the pavement along the **Hollywood Walk of Fame,** Hollywood Boulevard between Gower Street and La Brea Avenue; and Vine Street, between Yucca Street and Sunset Boulevard (✆ **323/469-8311;** www.hollywoodchamber. net). John Lennon, Elvis Presley, and Eddie Murphy, those were medallions worth a snapshot or two.

But why settle for sidewalk plaques when you can see films really being made? A quick prefab version is the hour-long tram tour at **Universal Studios Hollywood,** Hollywood Freeway, Universal Center Drive or Lankershim Boulevard exits, Universal City (✆ **818/ 622-3801;** www.universalstudioshollywood.com), but these days thrill rides are more Universal's raison d'être. We'd rather walk around the wardrobe and prop departments, backlots, and active sets of a real working studio. These walking tours run Monday through Friday and last 2 hours or more; advance reservations are essential. Here are your options: **Paramount Pictures,** 5555 Melrose Ave. (✆ 323/956-1777); **Warner Brothers Studios,** WB Studio Gate 3, 3400 Riverside Drive, Burbank (✆ 818/972-TOUR; www. wbstudiotour.com; ages 9 and up); **Sony Pictures,** 10202 W. Washington Blvd., Culver City (✆ 310/244-TOUR; www.sonypictures studios.com; ages 12 and up); and **NBC Studios,** 3000 W. Alameda Ave., Burbank (✆ 818/840-3537; www.studioaudiences.com).

Or you can get free tickets to join the studio audience for a sitcom or talk show taping (however, many shows don't admit children under the age of 10 or even 18). For these, contact well in advance: **Audiences Unlimited, Inc.** (✆ 818/753-3470; www.tv tickets.com); **TVTIX.COM** (✆ 818/985-8811; www.tvtix.com); **CBS Television City,** 7800 Beverly Blvd. (✆ 323/575-2458); **NBC Studios,** 3000 W. Alameda Ave., Burbank (✆ 818/840-3537); **Paramount Studios** (✆ 323/956-1777); or **Universal Studios** (✆ 800/UNIVER-SAL; www.universalstudios.com).

ⓘ **Hollywood Visitor Information Center,** 6801 Hollywood Blvd. (✆ **323/467-6412;** www.discoverlosangeles.com)

✈ ⌨ See Griffith Observatory **63**.

WHY THEY'LL THANK YOU: Seeing stars.

Newport's Mansions
The Gilded Age Elite's Summer "Cottages"

Ages 7 & up • Newport, Rhode Island

DRIVING AROUND NEWPORT, RHODE ISLAND, YOU CAN'T HELP BUT GAWK at the turn-of-the-century mansions—Italianate *palazzi,* Tudor-style manors, faux French châteaux, all set in elegant formal landscaping, with imposing gates or walls to keep out the hoi polloi (for example, *you*). It's incredible to imagine the sort of wealth that built these homes, even more incredible to realize that these were just these families' summer houses (offhandedly referred to as mere "cottages").

While many of these houses are still private property, nine are open to the public for guided tours, popular with tourists year-round (though not all are open daily in winter). Don't cram too many into 1 day—the sheer opulence of these interiors can soon bring on sensory overload. The most popular is the **Breakers,** Ochre Point Avenue (✆ **401/847-1000**), a 70-room 1895 mansion designed for Commodore Vanderbilt by Richard Morris Hunt. Patterned after Renaissance Florentine *palazzi,* it has a stunning great hall, an ornate 50-foot cube sheathed in marble. The Breakers even has bathrooms (very high-tech for the time) where both fresh and salt water come out of the taps. Stanford White modeled **Rosecliff,** Bellevue Avenue (✆ **401/847-1000**), after the Grand Trianon at Versailles. Built in 1902 for an heiress of the Comstock Lode mining fortune, it has only 40 rooms (how sad), but it also has Newport's largest ballroom and a heart-shaped grand staircase. **Beechwood,** 580 Bellevue Ave. (✆ **401/846-3772**), was built for the famous Mrs. Astor, who personally maintained a list of who counted and who didn't in New York and Newport society. Kids will especially like this house because actors in period dress are on hand to tell anecdotes about late Victorian high society.

The Breakers in Newport.

Two other Bellevue Avenue houses belonged to the same woman—named Alva Vanderbilt when she was mistress of **Marble House,** 596 Bellevue Ave. (✆ **401/847-1000**), so called because it shows off just about every type of marble there is. Its ballroom is literally dazzling, with three kinds of gold encrusting its walls. Alva divorced her Vanderbilt husband and promptly married his best friend, who was a Belmont and lived down the street at **Belcourt Castle,** 657 Bellevue Ave. (✆ **401/846-0669**). My daughter couldn't get over the luxurious stables. The Breakers may have had bathrooms, but Belcourt Castle had electricity, designed by Thomas Edison, no less. Tell the kids to look for the 14 secret doors.

ⓘ **Preservation Society of Newport,** 424 Bellevue Ave. (✆ **401/ 847-1000;** www.newportmansions.org)

✈ Providence, 28 miles

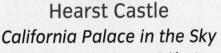

$$$ Hyatt Regency Newport, 1 Goat Island (© **888/591-1234** or 401/851-1234; http://newport.hyatt.com). $$ **Mill Street Inn,** 75 Mill St. (© **800/392-1316** or 401/849-9500; www.millstreet inn.com).

BEST TIME: Dec, when the houses are decorated for the holidays.

WHY THEY'LL THANK YOU: Imagine sliding down these banisters.

Castles & Mansions **72**

Hearst Castle
California Palace in the Sky
Ages 8 & up • San Simeon, California

IT'S NOT ENTIRELY TRUE THAT THE HILLTOP CALIFORNIA ESTATE OF publishing magnate William Randolph Hearst is a 20th-century replica of an Old World manor. True, it was built from 1919 to 1947, but the bits and pieces are nearly all authentic—400-year-old Spanish and Italian ceilings, 500-year-old mantels, 16th-century Florentine bedsteads, Renaissance paintings, Flemish tapestries, and innumerable other European treasures, which Hearst compulsively acquired for years.

Each week, railroad cars carrying fragments of Roman temples, carved doors from Italian monasteries, hastily rolled canvases by the old masters, ancient Persian rugs, and antique French furniture arrived—5 tons at a time—in San Simeon. Orson Welles's 1941 masterpiece *Citizen Kane,* a thinly disguised fictional biography of Hearst, has an unforgettable shot of priceless antiques warehoused in dusty piles, stretching as far as the eye can see. Only a fraction of what Hearst bought was ever installed in the estate.

Despite this patchwork approach, this sprawling Mediterranean Revival–style compound has a unified look, no doubt because one

Hearst Castle.

architect (and a woman at that, Julia Morgan) directed its entire 28-year creation. The main house, **Casa Grande,** alone has more than 100 rooms of baronial splendor. My kids lusted after the red-velvet-padded private movie theater where Hearst (also a movie mogul) screened first-run films. They longed to jump into the fabulous swimming pools—a Roman-inspired indoor pool with intricate mosaics, and the breathtaking outdoor Greco-Roman Neptune pool, flanked by marble colonnades that frame the distant sea.

Book your **guided tour** in advance if possible—there's not much else around this stretch of California coast, so Hearst Castle doesn't cater to drop-in business (everybody staying at our motel had either been there that day or was going tomorrow). You'll park down at the visitor center and take a bus uphill to the compound. Four different daytime tours visit various parts of the estate, with very little overlap; they last about 2 hours. Tour 1 covered all the essentials my kids wanted, but I regretted not seeing Hearst's private library and Gothic bedroom, which were on Tour 2. Too bad the **evening tours** were full when we booked—for those, costumed docents portray Hearst's celebrity house party guests. Thanks to Hearst's mistress, actress Marion Davies, the estate was a playground for the Hollywood crowd.

ⓘ 750 Hearst Castle Rd. (ⓒ **805/927-2020** or 800/444-4445 for tour reservations; www.hearstcastle.org)

✈ Monterey Peninsula, 94 miles

🛏 $$ **Best Western Cavalier Oceanfront Resort,** 9415 Hearst Dr. (ⓒ **800/826-8168** or 805/927-4688; www.cavalierresort.com)

WHY THEY'LL THANK YOU: Versailles-scale opulence for an American Sun King.

The Mark Twain Home
Tom Sawyer's Stomping Grounds
Ages 6 & up • Hannibal, Missouri

WHEN YOU ROLL INTO THIS LAID-BACK RIVER TOWN, ABOUT 130 MILES UP
the scenic Mississippi river road from St. Louis, you may get a nag-
ging feeling that you've been here before. Well, you have—if
you've read *The Adventures of Tom Sawyer*. Every scene in that
book was based on affectionate memories of the town where a boy
named Sam Clemens grew up, long before he became Mark Twain.
Sometimes Hannibal leans on the association a bit too much—
every third restaurant or shop seems to be named after a Tom
Sawyer character—but the historic heart of town really does have
a remarkable connection to this beloved American writer.

Eight properties around town, packaged under the name the Mark
Twain Museum, have rock-solid associations with Sam Clemens.
The main one is the small white frame house at 208 Hill St. where
the Clemens family lived from 1844 to 1853; the parlor, the dining
room, the kitchen, and the three upstairs bedrooms are all furnished in the period. You can almost imagine Sam climbing out the
window of the back bedroom he shared with his brother Henry,
sneaking off to nighttime escapades. Across the street is the much
more prosperous house of the Hawkins family, whose daughter
Laura—Twain's lifelong friend—was the model for Becky Thatcher.
The law office of Sam's father, John Clemens, has been moved to
the same street; its tiny front courtroom was the setting for Muff
Potter's trial in *Tom Sawyer*. After a shift in the family fortunes, the
Clemenses moved to cramped quarters above the old-fashioned
pharmacy run by Dr. Orville Grant, over on Main Street. The last
stop on this historic trail may not be authentic, but it could be the
kids' favorite: the **Museum Gallery,** set in an old department store
on Main Street, where interactive displays on *Tom Sawyer* allow

children to whitewash a fence, hide in a spooky graveyard, and get lost in a cave, just like Tom and Huck and Becky did.

Of all the peripheral attractions in town, the one that has the most true Tom-'n'-Huck flavor is the **Mark Twain Cave,** a mile south of town on U.S. 79. Whether or not Sam Clemens actually got lost during a school picnic in either of these two caves, it's easy to imagine him making mischief down here, and the guides on the 1-hour tour are sure to work in references to the book.

Sleepy as Hannibal seems most of the year, it crackles to life during the **National Tom Sawyer Days,** the long weekend around July 4. All sorts of Twain-themed activities are held outdoors, from fence painting to frog jumping, and it's just generally the sort of whoop-de-do that Sam Clemens—or Tom Sawyer—would have loved.

ⓘ ☏ **573/221-9010;** www.marktwainmuseum.org

✈ Lambert–St. Louis International, 125 miles

🛏 $ **Hannibal Travelodge,** 500 Mark Twain Ave. (☏ **800/578-7878** or 573/221-4100; www.hannibaltravelodge.com). $$ **Hotel Clemens,** 401 N. Third St. (☏ **573/248-1150;** www.hotelclemens. us).

WHY THEY'LL THANK YOU: Channeling an idyllic small-town childhood.

U.S. Presidents

74

The Lincoln Trail
From a Log Cabin to the White House
All ages • Multiple sites

EVEN BEFORE HIS ASSASSINATION, ABRAHAM LINCOLN WAS A REVERED President, the hero who steered America through the Civil War. Long before the modern mania for historical preservation, sites associated with Lincoln were turned into memorials. For kids, however, it's important to peel away the layers of myth to find the flesh-and-blood Lincoln. Drive the Lincoln Trail through Kentucky, Indiana, and Illinois and you'll find the backwoods boy behind the great President.

There's something bizarre about the first stop, in Hodgenville, Kentucky, the **Abraham Lincoln Birthplace National Historic Site,** where a huge neoclassical memorial encloses a tiny log cabin, reportedly the one where Lincoln was born on February 12, 1809. You'll get a better sense of Lincoln's humble origins 7 miles north of town on Highway 31E at **Lincoln's Boyhood Home,** where he spent ages 2 to 7; though the log cabin here is a reconstruction, its rough log walls and split-rail fences truly evoke a hardscrabble Kentucky childhood.

Cross the Ohio River, taking I-65 north and then I-64 west, a 135-mile drive to Lincoln City, Indiana. The Lincoln family cleared 20 acres here in 1816, when Abe was 7, and farmed the land for 14 years as he grew to manhood. If the boy Abe Lincoln comes to life anywhere on the trail, it's at the **Lincoln Boyhood National Memorial:** A symbolic bronze hearth and foundations mark the actual site of the Lincoln cabin; a living history farm (open late Apr to Oct) re-creates early-19th-century farm life; and you can walk a trail to the grave of Nancy Hanks Lincoln, whose death so grieved her 9-year-old son. The Memorial itself is a bit pompous, but the rooms inside strike a note of pioneer simplicity.

The next leg of your drive is about 250 miles, up to Springfield, Illinois, where the adult Lincoln really began to make his mark. The **Abraham Lincoln Presidential Library** is the snazzy centerpiece to Springfield's Lincoln worship, with loads of important artifacts (including a handwritten copy of the Gettysburg address), dioramas of his log cabin, parts of the White House, and the Ford's Theater box where he was shot. In town, you can visit the **Lincoln Home,** 426 S. 7th St., and a 4-block historic area around it, as well as his old **law office,** 209 S. 6th St., and the stately **Lincoln's Tomb.** But also squeeze in a 20-mile side trip northwest on Route 97 to the restored prairie village of **New Salem,** where from 1831 to 1837 young lawyer Abraham boarded at the Rutledge Tavern and fell in love with the innkeeper's daughter Ann, who died at 21. Some say Abe never got over her—ah, there's the human side of Lincoln again.

ⓘ **Abraham Lincoln Birthplace National Historic Site,** 2995 Lincoln Farm Rd., Hodgenville, KY (✆ **270/358-3137;** www.nps. gov/abli). **Lincoln Boyhood National Memorial,** 2916 E. South St., Lincoln City, IN (✆ **812/937-4541;** www.nps.gov/libo). **Abraham Lincoln Presidential Library,** 112 N. 6th St., Springfield, IL (✆ **217/558-8848;** www.alplm.org).

✈ Standiford Field, Louisville, KY, 45 miles from Hodgenville. Capital Airport, Springfield, IL.

🛏 $ **Baymont Inn,** 6 S. Washington St., Dale, IN (✆ **800/301-0200** or 812/937-7000; www.baymontdalein.com). $$ **Mansion View Inn,** 529 S. 4th St., Springfield, IL (✆ **800/252-1083** or 217/544-7411; www.mansionview.com). $$$ **Seelbach Hilton,** 500 4th St., Louisville, KY (✆ **502/585-3200;** www.seelbachhilton.com).

WHY THEY'LL THANK YOU: Seeing the modest beginnings of an American icon.

U.S. Presidents

75

Franklin & Eleanor Roosevelt's Homes
How America's First Power Couple Summered
Ages 8 & up • Hyde Park, New York

FRANKLIN DELANO ROOSEVELT AND HIS COUSIN ELEANOR, WHO LATER became his wife, grew up in New York's Hudson River Valley, where wealthy families like the Vanderbilts had colossal summer homes, so it was natural they'd have a home there even after they became President and First Lady. In fact, they had not one home but three, for both Franklin and Eleanor both had separate getaway cottages on the estate, where they could escape the pressures of political life. To visit these three homes in 1 afternoon is to get a powerful sense of this great American couple.

Franklin Roosevelt's lifelong home, **Springwood,** was a modest farmhouse when FDR's father built it. Franklin expanded it in an eclectic Dutch colonial style, giving it an imposing red-brick porticoed facade—my kids would call it a mansion, but it isn't by any means as grand as the great river estates nearby. Nevertheless, FDR entertained Winston Churchill, King George VI and Queen Elizabeth of England, and many other dignitaries here. He also designed his own presidential library, the nation's first, while still in his second term. Of all the presidential libraries this is the one that feels warmed by a chief executive's presence—you see his cluttered White House desk, left as it was the last day of his presidency, and his beloved 1936 Ford Phaeton with the hand controls that enabled him to drive all over the estate. FDR and Eleanor are buried in the rose garden on the grounds.

A wooded trail leads from Springwood to the pair of private retreats. Simple, rustic **Val-Kill Cottage** was Eleanor's haven, especially after FDR's death in 1945. This flagstone cottage was in fact the only home she ever owned herself. Shy, awkward Eleanor rose to become one of the most influential women of her time, making her mark on civil rights legislation and international humanitarian issues (as a U.N. delegate, she chaired the committee that drafted the U.N. Human Rights Universal Declaration), and she met with many world leaders here at homey Val-Kill. The grounds were also the headquarters of Val-Kill Industries, which Eleanor and several other women established to teach trades to rural workers and produce colonial revival furniture and crafts.

FDR built his hilltop retreat, **Top Cottage,** in the 1930s, while his work as President included battling the Great Depression. FDR was at his most relaxed here, even allowing himself to be photographed in his wheelchair. Though the cottage is unfurnished today, you can go out onto the porch and appreciate his cherished views of the Catskill and Shawangunk Mountains. Imagine what it was like in 1939, when FDR hosted Churchill and the king and queen of England to a hot dog dinner on the porch.

ⓘ **FDR,** 4079 Albany Post Rd., off Rte. 9 (ⓒ **800/FDR-VISIT** or 845/229-8114; www.nps.gov/hofr or www.fdrlibrary.marist.edu). **Eleanor Roosevelt,** Rte. 9G (ⓒ **845/486-7770;** www.nps.gov/elro).

🚃 Poughkeepsie, 8 miles

🛏 $$ **Journey Inn,** 1 Sherwood Place, Hyde Park (© **845/229-8972;** www.journeyinn.com)

WHY THEY'LL THANK YOU: Two American history icons become human here.

Hiking & Camping **76**

Yosemite: Rock-Climbing Heaven
Ages 8 & up • Yosemite, California, USA

MOST FOLKS VISITING YOSEMITE NATIONAL PARK DON'T SEEM TO REALize that there's more to it than Yosemite Valley, where crowds of cars and RVs inch along the roads while their passengers stare at the 3,000-foot-high glacier-carved granite walls and the waterfalls that drop down them. Yes, you should drive past the awesome 7,549-foot-high sheer rock face called El Capitan; you should pull off the road to take the easy half-mile trails to view Bridalveil Fall or Lower Yosemite Falls. But don't stop there—go up into the high country, where you can explore wilderness without the crowds.

The eastern half of 39-mile-long **Tioga Road** is open only in summer and fall, and the developed area around **Tuolumne Meadows** is much less crowded than Yosemite Valley; there's even a grove of sequoias, where you can enjoy the gigantic trees in much greater peace than you'll have at larger Mariposa Grove, near the park's south entrance. Coming from the west, Tioga Road rises up through towering pines and then breaks out on solid granite highlands dramatically furrowed by glaciers. Around Olmsted Point, the views become really dramatic—look at a cliff jutting up in the distance, and you'll realize that the ants scaling it are actually rock climbers. Yosemite is the most popular rock-climbing destination in the United States, thanks largely to the **Yosemite Mountaineering School** (© **209/372-8344;** www.yosemitemountaineering. com). The climbing school runs beginner classes daily out of its base in popular Curry Village, but in summer you can also take classes at Tuolumne Meadows. Kids as young as 14 are accepted,

Best Things to Do in Yosemite National Park

- Hike over the bedrock high country to see unbelievable scenery.
- Play in the streams of Yosemite Valley or Wawona.
- See the high waterfalls and cliffs of Yosemite Valley and the giant sequoias of the Merced Grove.
- Backpack in the cool, spectacular mountains.
- Try cross-country skiing or snowshoeing in the winter.

and the instructors will soon have your teenagers inching up the granite walls to heights of 60 feet.

Even children who are too young to scale a sheer rock face can get a little climbing experience in Yosemite's high country. From Tuolumne Meadows Lodge, a 4.2-mile trail leads to the top of **Lembert Dome** (take a shuttle bus back to the lodge from the trail's other end). Another option is off of Glacier Point Road, south of the Yosemite Valley loop. You'll want to drive this road anyway to get to that great Glacier Point overlook, the top of a 3,200-foot vertical cliff. But stop partway along Glacier Point Road at mile 13.2, where a trail head leads 2.2 miles round-trip to **Sentinel Dome,** one of many granite domes in the park whose rounded shapes were formed by glaciers moving over them. It's 8,122 feet high, the second-highest viewpoint into the valley. **Taft Point** is the same distance the other way from the trail head; it has weird and scary cracks as well as cliff-overhang views. The hike itself isn't threatening, but hold hands near the end.

ⓘ Entrances on CA 41, CA 120, and CA 140 (ⓒ **209/372-0200;** www.nps.gov/yose)

✈ Fresno-Yosemite International, 90 miles

🛏 $$$ **The Ahwahnee,** Yosemite Valley (ⓒ **801/559-5000**). $ **Tuolumne Meadows Campground** (ⓒ **800/436-7275;** www. reservations.gov).

WHY THEY'LL THANK YOU: Being on those peaks, not just looking at them.

Walking the Appalachian Trail
Ages 8 & up • White Mountains, New Hampshire

FOR THE ULTIMATE FAMILY BONDING ADVENTURE, NOTHING QUITE equals a hike along the Appalachian Trail. No, I'm not suggesting you do the whole rugged 2,100 miles of the Trail, which runs from Maine to Georgia. But you can conquer a segment of it, and one I'd recommend runs 56 miles through the White Mountain National Forest, where the nonprofit **Appalachian Mountain Club (AMC)** runs a unique network of eight huts, each a day's walk apart. Providing food and bedding, they let you travel light, reduced to backpacking essentials: some warm clothes, foul-weather gear, water, snacks. You'll be amid some of the most spectacular scenery in the East—no trash, trailers, or loud music (the curse of overcrowded national park campgrounds), just room for kids to explore the world with new friends, kicking dust, balancing on fallen trees, and learning that when it rains you can't always change the channel.

My personal favorite family hike is a 3-day excursion up **Mount Lafayette.** Begin on the Franconia Notch Parkway (Rte. 93), about 7¹/₂ miles north of Lincoln, New Hampshire, where you'll find the signpost for the Old Bridle Path trail head. It's a sometimes-steep 2.9-mile hike from the road to the Greenleaf Hut, just above timberline at 4,200 feet, a warm, friendly place on Lafayette's west slope. When we last visited, the cook banged a pot with a heavy metal spoon at 6pm sharp, and we joined about 25 others—a lively mingling of singles, couples, and families—at long wooden tables for a very honest chicken-and-vegetable stew, with homemade bread and a mysterious pudding. After dinner, we sat on a rocky ledge and watched the evening mist flow through the valley below.

Next morning is your main hiking day: Climb 1.1 miles to the rocky, often windswept summit of Mount Lafayette. The payoff, on clear days, is the 1.7-mile (1-hr.) walk from Lafayette along a narrow ridge, with the whole Franconia range stretched below you, to Little Haystack. Retrace your steps to the Greenleaf Hut for your second night. On the morning of the third day, return to your car, an easy 2-hour downhill hike.

Other AMC huts that are popular with families are at **Zealand Falls,** a 2.8-mile walk to a choice four-season spot near waterfalls, perfect for moose spotting; and the even more accessible **Lonesome Lake Hut,** a painless 1.7-mile hike to a lake. Guided hut-to-hut trips can also be arranged.

(**i**) ✆ **603/528-8721;** www.fs.fed.us/r9/forests/white_mountain

✈ Logan Airport, Boston, MA

⊨ Contact **Appalachian Mountain Club** (✆ **603/466-2727;** www.outdoors.org)

WHY THEY'LL THANK YOU: The joy of reaching the summit—together.

---

78 **Hiking & Camping**

Getting Past the Crowds in Yellowstone

All ages • Entrances at Gardiner & West Yellowstone Montana & Jackson & Cody Wyoming

YELLOWSTONE NATIONAL PARK IS ONE OF THE COUNTRY'S BEST PLACES for families to go backpacking. Some beautiful campsites are just a couple miles off the road, and it only takes a walk of 20 minutes or so before you feel gloriously alone with the bison, elk, and other wildlife.

Yellowstone National Park.

Every visitor to Yellowstone wants to see the park's signature attraction, the Old Faithful geyser, which erupts about every 90 minutes. You can drive to Old Faithful on the Lower Loop Road from the park's west entrance and join the crowds of tourists sitting on benches waiting for this baby to blow. Another popular drive-up sight is the limestone terraces of **Mammoth Hot Springs,** near the north entrance, where masses of bacteria and algae in the thermal water turn the rocks orange, pink, yellow, green, and brown. But these two sights only scratch the surface of Yellowstone's geothermal features. You'll have the geysers practically to yourself if you head for the **Shoshone Geyser Basin,** which begins a mile west of Shoshone Lake (find a trail head for Delacey Creek Trail on the road 8 miles east of Old Faithful; it leads 3 miles to Shoshone Lake). The North Shoshone Trail passes 26 campsites as it winds through a lodgepole-pine forest. The **Bechler Meadows Trail** in the park's southwest corner is rich in waterfalls, cascades, and thermal areas. If it's wildlife you're after, try the **Sportsman Lake Trail,** which passes through sagebrush plateaus full of elk and a meadow popular with moose.

Some great family trails for day hikes include these: at Mammoth, the 5-mile **Beaver Ponds Loop** from the hot springs at Liberty Cap (go in the evening or early morning to see the beavers); the 6-mile round-trip hike up **Mount Washburn,** an alpine trail leading to a 10,243-foot-high view over much of Yellowstone (watch for bighorn sheep); and the **Clear Lake trail** from the Wapiti Trailhead, which wanders through beautiful rolling meadows to a strange body of water fed by hot springs.

The backcountry season here is short—mid-June through the end of August, when the snow has finally melted off and streams drop to fordable levels. Contact the **Yellowstone Backcountry Office** (✆ **307/344-2160**); their *Backcountry Trip Planner* details the process for getting permits and includes a map pinpointing all campsites. In peak season, it's wise to make a reservation in advance.

ⓘ ✆ **307/344-7381;** www.nps.gov/yell

✈ West Yellowstone Airport, 2 miles. Yellowstone Regional Airport, Cody, WY, 52 miles.

🛏 $ **Madison Hotel,** 139 Yellowstone Ave., West Yellowstone (✆ **800/838-7745** or 406/646-7745, www.madisonhotelmotel. com). $$ **Mammoth Hot Springs Hotel** (✆ **866/439-7375;** www. travelyellowstone.com).

WHY THEY'LL THANK YOU: Learning to tell an elk from a moose.

79   Cycling

Bicycling on Nantucket

All ages • Nantucket, Massachusetts

BRINGING A CAR TO NANTUCKET, THE TINY MASSACHUSETTS ISLAND 30 miles off Cape Cod, can be an incredible hassle in summer—there are only six pokey car ferries per day from Hyannis, and they book up months in advance. Day visitors generally choose to come on foot (which frees you to opt for a high-speed ferry), but then they don't explore any further than tourist-mobbed Nantucket Town. Your solution? Rent bikes. Flat, sandy Nantucket is heaven for beginning bicyclists, with paved paths leading all over. Bring helmets with you (they're required for children under 12) or rent them along with bikes in Nantucket Town at shops right by the wharf. Nothing could be easier, or more fun.

Here's the lay of the land: Three major bike routes radiate out from Nantucket Town, one heading west to Madaket, 6¼ miles, one south to Surfside 3½ miles, and the longest one a 17-mile loop out to Siasconset Beach ('Sconset to locals) and Sankaty Head lighthouse. It's classic beachy terrain, with few trees, wide skies, and swaths of tall dune grass on both sides. The pedaling is easy, and the island's small scale makes you feel you're really getting somewhere, especially when you hit the bluffs and get that Atlantic panorama. Picnic benches and water fountains are conveniently provided at strategic points along all the paths, which you'll appreciate if you're towing really young ones in a bike trailer.

Madaket is picturesque, especially at sunset, but has strong surf; with kids, you're better off turning right on Eel Point Road and swimming at gentler Dionis Beach. Popular **Surfside** beach is your best bet with young children, not only because the ride is shorter but because there's a snack bar. My favorite, though, is the ride to **'Sconset,** even though it is the most demanding, longer and with a few hills. 'Sconset is rarely, if ever, crowded, perhaps because of the water's strong sideways tow. Lifeguards are usually on duty, but the closest facilities (restrooms, grocery store, and cafe) are back in the center of the village, which is lovely and worth a stop anyway. From 'Sconset, head north along the coastal path on Polpis Road, stopping off to snap Nantucket photos in front of the classic lighthouse at Sankaty Head. If you've planned ahead, though, you've booked an unforgettable naturalist-led tour (offered June–Oct) of the barrier beaches with the **Coskata-Coatue Wildlife Refuge (© 508/228-6799;** reservation required); detour up Wauwinet Road to the Wauwinet Inn to meet the tour. By the time you pedal back into Nantucket Town and get back on the ferry, you'll have spent a day in the sun you won't soon forget.

(i) **Nantucket Visitor Services,** 25 Federal St. (© **508/228-0925;** www.nantucket-ma.gov)

✈ Nantucket Airport

🛏 **Jared Coffin House,** 29 Broad St., Nantucket (© **800/248-2405** or 508/228-2400; www.jaredcoffinhouse.com)

WHY THEY'LL THANK YOU: A first taste of bike touring that'll leave them wanting more.

80 Cycling

Cycling the Rim Road: Crater Lake

Ages 8 & up • Crater Lake, Oregon

THE STORY BEGINS WITH A VOLCANIC EXPLOSION SO FEARSOME— scientists estimate it was 42 times as powerful as Mount St. Helens—that it left behind a phenomenally deep crater, which in time filled with water to become America's deepest lake. But this version of events doesn't prepare you for the sight of Crater Lake, for the intense sapphire blue of its cold spring-fed waters reflecting the sheer forested cliffs that encircle it. It's simply breathtaking, a panorama of supreme serenity that belies its violent origins. It takes about 2 hours to drive around Crater Lake—which, unfortunately, is all most park visitors do, rolling along the asphalt, narcotized by the pretty scenery. Trade in those four wheels for two, though, and you'll really feel the transforming power of this volcanic landscape.

The 33-mile **Rim Drive,** open only in summer, has 30 overlooks where you can gaze at these pristine waters cupped in their rocky chalice. Travel clockwise, wear bright clothing so motorists can spot you, and if possible sleep in the park the night before so you can hit the narrow road early before the traffic gets heavy (as it inevitably will). The Rim Drive may look like an easy pedal, but don't underestimate it—it can be demanding, especially on the east side of the lake, where there are more hills (hills you'd scarcely notice if you were just driving). On the other hand, the east side of the lake has more panoramic views, providing good excuses to catch your breath. The **Cloudcap Overlook** is 2,000 feet high, with vistas that stretch as far as Mount Shasta. Another cool turnoff overlooks the **Phantom Ship,** a jagged basalt formation jutting up out of the lake.

An alternative ride goes from the Rim Village visitor center north to the **Cleetwood Cove Trailhead** and back, 21 miles total, on the flatter west rim. Cleetwood Cove is the sole trail that goes down to the lake's edge; it may only be 2.2 miles round-trip, but the way back is strenuous, like climbing 65 flights of stairs. My advice: Save your strength for the cycling.

No matter which of the park's entrances you come in, you'll drive a few miles to get to the Rim Drive, where you can park your car and get the bikes off your rack. If you've got more than one driver in your party, consider taking turns driving the car to meet the cyclists at each overlook—it'll give the kids the option of pooping out if necessary. (Blame it on the high altitude.) There are no bike rentals in the park, but you can rent them at **Diamond Lake Resort,** 5 miles from the park's north entrance on State Road 138.

ⓘ Along OR 62 (ℭ **541/594-3000;** www.nps.gov/crla)

✈ Rogue Valley International, Medford, OR, 71 miles

🛏 $$$ **Crater Lake Lodge,** Rim Rd. (ℭ **541/830-8700** or 888/774-2728; www.craterlakelodges.com). $ **Mazama Village Campground,** in the park off OR 62 (www.craterlakelodges.com/Mazama-Village-Campground-815.html).

BEST TIME: Late June to Sept.

WHY THEY'LL THANK YOU: Discovering how rugged this pretty place really is.

81

The Grand Canyon
The Mules Know the Way
Ages 7 & up • Arizona

WHILE IT'S AWESOME INDEED TO STAND ON THE RIM OF THE GRAND Canyon and drink in its resplendent panoramas, something about that monumental chasm makes me long to just *dive in.* Any number of hiking trails lead down into this great natural wonder, raft trips ply its waters, and helicopters buzz overhead—but surely the most memorable way to explore the Grand Canyon is to pick your way down the steep, narrow trails on the back of an ornery mule. Let the trail-wise mules find their footing on the stony paths while you gaze around you, drinking in the unfolding vistas of this vast network of canyons.

The best options for kids depart from the North Rim and are offered by **Canyon Trail Rides** (© **928/638-9875;** www.canyon rides.com). Children as young as 7 can try out the mules on a 1-hour scenic ride along the rim; at 10 years and up, they can do half-day trips, either a longer rim route or one that heads 2,300 feet down the North Kaibab Trail, along a dramatic series of switchbacks through thick forest to the Supai Tunnel. If the kids are 12, they can take a full day trip, going 4,300 feet down and back up the North Kaibab Trail through a terrain of bright red rocks to Roaring Springs (aptly named—you'll hear it well before you reach it).

From the South Rim, the shortest possible excursion is a 12-mile day trip to Plateau Point, an overlook of the Colorado River rushing 1,300 feet below. The real classics, though, are 1- or 2-night packages that go to the bottom of the canyon and include sleeping arrangements and simple meals at **Phantom Ranch,** the only lodging available below the rim of the Grand Canyon. Don't expect luxury—it's all bunk-bedded cabins and dorms, connected by dirt

Best Things to Do at the Grand Canyon

- **See the canyon at dawn or sunset,** when the angle of the sun picks out the folds in the rock.
- **Rise before dawn to hike** at least a little way down into the canyon, seeing how its extraordinary walls look from close up.
- **Get a backcountry camping permit** so that you can hike farther, away from the crowds.

footpaths and shaded by cottonwood trees, set half a mile north of the Colorado River. All the same, it's more than you might have expected to find down here. These Phantom Ranch trips are so popular, they fill up as soon as reservations are accepted, 23 months in advance (call ☏ **888/297-2757** for reservations). For possible openings the next day, call the Bright Angel Transportation Desk at ☏ **928/638-2631,** ext. 6015. There's no age restriction per se, but riders must be at least 4 feet 7 inches tall; pregnant women are not allowed.

ⓘ ☏ **800/638-7888;** www.nps.gov/grca

✈ Grand Canyon National Park Airport, Tusayan, AZ

🛏 $$$ **El Tovar Hotel,** South Rim (☏ **928/638-2631**). $$ **Grand Canyon Lodge,** North Rim (☏ **877/386-4383**).

WHY THEY'LL THANK YOU: Discovering what's in that hole in the ground.

Canoeing the Everglades
Paddling Through a River of Grass
Ages 6 & up • Florida City or Everglades City, Florida

THE EVERGLADES IS A BIZARRE ECOSYSTEM, WHEN YOU THINK ABOUT IT: a drawling grassy river that's rarely more than knee-deep, but spreads some 40 miles wide, harboring an exotic population of manatees, hawksbill turtles, water moccasins, coral snakes, panthers, armadillos, muskrats, opossums, river otters, herons, egrets, the roseate spoonbill, and the big black anhinga bird. It's the only place in the world where alligators and crocodiles live side by side. There's nothing like it anywhere else—and it might not be here much longer, given the encroaching development in southern Florida. Bring the kids here now, to dip a paddle into this River of Grass while it still flows.

While you can stick to dry land—driving or biking on the paved park roads, or walking short nature trails through junglelike patches of forest—the whole point of this place is that it *isn't* dry land. What you really want is to feel the sway and lap of the park's waters, the lazy grace of its fluid meander through mangroves and cypresses and sawgrass prairies. Rent canoes at the **Gulf Coast visitor center** in Everglades City or the **Flamingo Lodge** by the Flamingo visitor center at the southern tip of the park. In a canoe you'll be incredibly close to the water level, casually coexisting with gators and birds as if you're part of their natural environment. That just won't happen on those powered airboats that offer Everglades tours just outside park boundaries. (They aren't allowed in the park proper.)

Everglades National Park's longest "trails" are designed for canoe travel, and many are marked as clearly as walking trails. From the Gulf Coast, you can canoe 2 miles across **Chokoloskee Bay** to a mangrove island, or follow the **Turner River** 8 miles from freshwater cypress forest into saltwater mangrove swamp. From

Everglades City, Florida.

Flamingo, the **Noble Hammock Canoe Trail** is an easy 2-mile loop; the **Hell's Bay Canoe Trail** is 3 to 6 miles, depending on how far you venture. A guided canoe tour is a great idea, not only to find your way but to benefit from the guide's familiarity with the flora and fauna; contact **Everglades National Park Boat Tours** (© **239/695-2591**) at the Parks Docks on Chokoloskee Causeway (Hwy. 29) in Everglades City, or **North American Canoe Tours** at the Ivey House (see below).

ⓘ **Ernest F. Coe Visitor Center,** Hwy. 9336, west of Florida City. **Gulf Coast Visitor Center,** Hwy. 29, Everglades City. **Flamingo Visitor Center,** end of Hwy. 9336 (© **305/242-7700;** www.nps.gov/ever).

 Miami International, 40 miles

🛏 **$$ Best Western Gateway to the Keys,** 411 S. Krome Ave. (U.S. 1), Florida City (☎ **305/246-5100;** www.bestwestern.com). **$$ Ivey House B&B,** 107 Camellia St., Everglades City (☎ **239/695-3299;** www.iveyhouse.com).

BEST TIME: Dry season (winter or spring).

WHY THEY'LL THANK YOU: Gliding through the glassy, grassy silence.

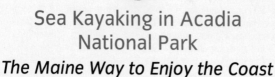

83 Paddling Away

Sea Kayaking in Acadia National Park
The Maine Way to Enjoy the Coast
Ages 8 & up • Mount Desert Island, Maine

MAINE'S MOUNT DESERT ISLAND IS HOME TO SPECTACULAR ACADIA National Park, a rich glacier-carved mound of rugged cliffs, restless ocean, and quiet woods. Mount Desert (pronounced des-*sert*) is surrounded by small bays and coast-hugging islands and nearly knifed in half by narrow, 7-mile-long Somes Sound, the only true fjord in the continental United States. Most visitors crowd onto 20-mile **Park Loop Road,** a spectacular drive that starts near the **Hulls Cove Visitor Center** and follows the rocky coast past picturesque coves, looping back inland along **Jordan Pond** and **Eagle Lake** with a detour to **Cadillac Mountain**—a sort of greatest-hits tour of the island. But why spend your time poking along in traffic, staring out at the ocean, when you could be skimming along the water's surface, skirting the coast and exploring the coves in your own light and agile sea kayak?

Frenchman's Bay, where the island's main town, **Bar Harbor**, sits, is a great place for youngsters to learn how to kayak, sitting in the front seat of a flat, stable two-person kayak with a parent paddling in back. Head south from the bay and you'll reach Atlantic waters, where popular park sights include **Thunder Hole**, a shallow cavern where the surf surges boisterously in and out, and **Otter Cliffs**, a set of 100-foot-high granite precipices capped with dense spruce that plummet down into roiling seas. From your kayak you can also enjoy open views of waterside villages and the great shingled "cottages" of the wealthy elite—Carnegies, Rockefellers, Astors, Vanderbilts—who summered here in the island's late-19th-century heyday as a resort.

Outfitters offer a variety of options, from a 2½-hour harbor tour to a 7-hour excursion. **Coastal Kayaking Tours,** 48 Cottage St., Bar Harbor (C 800/526-8615 or 207/288-9605; www.acadiafun. com), has a 4-hour outing tailored for families with children as young as 8. Experienced kayakers can set out on their own with rentals from **Loon Bay Kayaks,** Barcadia Campground, junction of Routes 3 and 102 (C 888/786-0676 or 207/667-2963), or **Aquaterra Adventures,** 1 West St., Bar Harbor (C 207/288-0007; www.aquaterra-adventures.com).

Frenchman's Bay is populated by seals, osprey, and other wildlife; in early fall, huge flocks of eider ducks can sometimes be seen floating just off the Atlantic shore. Summer boasts even more spectacular wildlife: humpback, finback, minke, and (occasionally) right whales, which migrate to cool summer waters offshore to feast on krill and plankton. For a closer look you can take an excursion with the **Bar Harbor Whale Watch Company,** 1 West St., Bar Harbor (C 888/533-WALE or 207/288-9800; barharborwhales.com).

ⓘ **Hulls Cove Visitor Center,** Rte. 3 (C **207/288-3338;** www. nps.gov/acad)

✈ Trenton, just across the causeway from Mount Desert Island

🛏 $ **Bar Harbor Campground,** 409 State Hwy. 3, Bar Harbor (C **207/288-5185**). $$$ **Harborside Hotel & Marina,** 55 West St., Bar Harbor (C **800/328-5033** or 207/288-5033; www.theharbor sidehotel.com).

WHY THEY'LL THANK YOU: Skimming over steel-blue seas, swift as an osprey.

Swimming with a Million Tiny Lights

Ages 4 & up • Vieques, Puerto Rico

I THOUGHT PUERTO RICO WAS AN ISLAND—BUT HOW CAN AN ISLAND have an island? Well, Puerto Rico has two, Vieques and Culebra, for years a well-kept secret among Puerto Ricans themselves, who come here to escape the tourists on the big island. Since the U.S. Navy in 2003 closed its installation on Vieques, though, much more land is available for vacationers, and Vieques is rapidly becoming known as an eco-friendly—and still charmingly scruffy—destination.

With some 40 palm-lined white-sand beaches, and reefs of snorkel-worthy antler coral off shore, Vieques—11km (6³/₄ miles) off the big island's east coast, only an hour by ferry—has an obvious appeal for sun-loving families. But one of the coolest things on Vieques has nothing at all to do with the sun. Just west of the main town, Isabel Segunda, lies **Mosquito Bay,** which has been renamed Phosphorescent Bay for the way its waters glow in the dark, thanks to millions of tiny bioluminescent organisms called pyrodiniums (translation from science-speak: "whirling fire"). They're only about one-five-hundredth of an inch in size, but when these tiny swimming creatures are disturbed (by, for example, a hovering tour boat), they dart away and light up like fireflies, leaving eerie blue-white trails of phosphorescence. These pyrodiniums exist elsewhere, but not in such amazing concentrations: A gallon of water in Mosquito Bay may contain upward of three-quarters of a million such creatures. It's definitely worth letting the kids stay up late for once. Wear a bathing suit because it's possible to swim in these glowing waters, a sensation the kids will find incredibly eerie and cool.

Don't make the mistake of coming here on a full moon, however—the glow of the pyrodiniums is only discernible on a cloudy, moon-less night. (**Warning:** Some tour boats go out to the bay regardless

A secluded beach on Vieques.

of the full moon—and you won't get your money back if you're disappointed.)

Island Adventures (☎ 787/741-0720) operates 2-hour nighttime trips in Phosphorescent Bay aboard the *Luminosa,* though not during the full moon. If the kids are into kayaking, they can get even closer to those glow-in-the-dark waters on a kayak tour offered by **Blue Caribe Kayak** (☎ 787/741-2522). In fact, Blue Caribe acts as a clearinghouse for all the island's watersports outfitters—it's a small island, and virtually everybody is related to everyone else. That small-town casualness is one of the things that still makes Vieques a great place for traveling families, hot spot or not.

ⓘ ☎ **787/721-2400;** www.gotopuertorico.com

✈ Vieques

🛏 $$ **Hacienda Tamarindo,** Rte. 996, Barrio Puerto Real (☎ **787/741-8525;** www.haciendatamarindo.com)

WHY THEY'LL THANK YOU: Nature's night light.

Biscayne National Park
Florida's Homegrown Coral Reef
Ages 8 & up • Homestead, Florida

BISCAYNE NATIONAL PARK IS ONE OF THE LEAST-CROWDED PARKS IN America's national park system, probably because its main attractions are kinda difficult to reach. It's not a question of being remote—it's so close to Miami, you can do it as a day trip—but more about being hidden from view. Aboveground, you'll see only a no-big-deal strip of mangrove shoreline and 44 barrier islands, most of them mere specks off of South Florida's east coast. But beneath the surface lies the world's third-longest coral reef, an aquatic universe pulsing with multicolored life. All it takes is strapping on a snorkel and fins for kids to be able to cruise around this tropical paradise, encountering bright parrotfish and angelfish, gently rocking sea fans, and coral labyrinths.

The clear, warm waters of Biscayne National Park are packed with reef fish, rays, moray eels, jellyfish, anemones, sponges, even sea turtles and dolphins—some 512 species, all told, in this 173,000-acre expanse. Not only that, an **underwater trail** identifies five shipwrecks about 3 miles east of Elliott Key; mooring buoys point the way to the wrecks, with waterproof cards attached to tell the kids what they're seeing. You can rent equipment at the full-service dive shop at the park's mainland entrance at Convoy Point, and if you don't have your own boat, you can take a 3-hour snorkeling or diving tour operated every afternoon by **Biscayne National Underwater Park, Inc.** (✆ **305/230-1100**); you'll either stick to the bay or head out to the reefs, depending on the very changeable weather. Even beginning snorkelers will get a satisfying eyeful.

The mainland entrance is 9 miles east of Homestead, off U.S. 1; a small beach and marina is nearby, but the rest of the park is accessible only by boat, either your own or the park concession's water transport (✆ **305/230-1100**). Few of the park's islands are even open to visitors; the two most popular are Elliott Key and Boca Chita Key, which can be reached by launch from the visitor center. Both islands have campsites (call the park ranger at ℂ **305/230-1144** for information on permits and camping fees) and places to moor your boat; **Elliott Key** also has an interesting nature trail, and **Boca Chita,** once an exclusive haven for yachters, has some restored historic buildings.

If you prefer not to dive, take the wimp's way out and view the underwater sights on a 3-hour **glass-bottom boat tour** offered by Biscayne National Underwater Park, Inc., departing from Convoy Point at 10am. Reservations are almost always necessary.

ⓘ **Dante Fascell Visitor Center,** at Convoy Point, 9700 SW 328th St. (ℂ **305/230-7275;** www.nps.gov/bisc)

✈ ⊨ See Miami Seaquarium ③⑨.

WHY THEY'LL THANK YOU: Tropical colors and eerie shipwrecks.

Snorkeling & Diving 86

St. John
Snorkeling on the Trunk Bay Trail
Ages 6 & up • St. John, U.S. Virgin Islands, the Caribbean

THE FIRST PLACE MY KIDS EVER PUT A MASK AND SNORKEL INTO THE water was down here in the U.S. Virgin Islands, and I'm afraid it spoiled them for more ordinary snorkeling experiences. I still have photos of them standing on the white-sand beach at Cinnamon Bay, along with the five kids of the other families we were traveling with, looking like an invasion party of aliens in their rented snorkeling gear—eight breathing tubes sticking up like antennae, eight pairs of flippers shifting impatiently in the sand, and their masks

The U.S. Virgin Islands.

making them look like eight frowning Cyclopes. We deliberately took forever getting that shot, just because it made them so antsy. Enough photos already, they wanted to get out in that turquoise water and *start snorkeling*.

Their snorkeling debuts took place where so many others have started out: at Trunk Bay, where the National Park Service has set up the **National Park Underwater Trail.** This 225-yard trail follows a reef where all the underwater features are labeled with signs 5 to 15 feet under the water's surface. Snorkeling snobs wouldn't be caught dead at popular Trunk Bay doing the trail—they prefer more remote places like Waterlemon Cay or Salt Pond Bay or Haulover Bay, where the snorkeling's a lot more challenging—but with children, Trunk Bay is just the thing. The signs help to focus young snorkelers' attention and keep them going, and it was extremely helpful for them to learn the difference between various coral structures, between a sea fan and an anemone. As for the bright parrotfish flitting by, well, no sign can be attached to something that elusive, but since the signs had made the kids more attentive snorkelers, they spotted the parrotfish all right. They were hoping for sea turtles—hawksbills and leatherbacks are common in these waters—but the turtles sensibly kept their distance. With kids, we were also grateful for Trunk Bay's other amenities—flush toilets, a snack bar, and lifeguards.

We also just plain fell in love with St. John—with two-thirds of it protected as Virgin Islands National Park, it's remarkably unspoiled, with lots of dense foliage and hiking trails and unruffled quiet, surrounded by expanses of clear, sparkling turquoise waters. It's what we'd always expected the Caribbean to be—and now that we had the kids hooked on snorkeling, our island-hopping days could begin.

ⓘ **Virgin Islands National Park**, Trunk Bay (✆ **340/776-6201**; www.nps.gov/viis)

✈ St. Thomas, 45–60 min. by boat

🛏 $$ **Cinnamon Bay Campground**, Cruz Bay (✆ **340/776-6330**; www.cinnamonbay.com). $$$ **Westin St. John Resort**, Great Cruz Bay (✆ **888/627-7206** or 340/693-8000; www.westin resortstjohn.com).

WHY THEY'LL THANK YOU: Connecting the dots underwater.

Beaches **87**

Santa Monica Beach
The Golden Essence of Beachy California
All ages • Santa Monica, California

Planning our most recent trip to Southern California, my kids envisioned a classic white-sand beach with the Pacific Ocean sparkling blue-green beyond and a gentle white-fringed surf they could jump in to their heart's content. It was ridiculously easy for us to fulfill that fantasy with a lazy afternoon at Santa Monica State Beach (off the Pacific Coast Hwy.). What's not to like? Even on a summer Sunday, this wide strand was blissfully uncrowded; restrooms, yes, tacky food stands, no. We could even bicycle up here on the paved beach path from funky Venice Beach, where the vibe is edgier but the sand and surf not nearly so nice. Santa Monica Beach has big parking lots and nearby cafes. It's one of those cases where hunting for the exotic is a waste of time: Santa Monica Beach is easy to get to, free, and sparkling clean, an ideal place for a quintessential California day at the beach.

Just south of the beach you can visit the **Santa Monica Pier,** Ocean Avenue at the end of Colorado Boulevard (⌀ **310/458-8900;** www. santamonicapier.org), one of the last of Southern California's vintage seaside piers. The Santa Monica Pier evokes the area's 19th-century seaside resort days, long before Los Angeles became La-La Land. Built in 1908 for passenger and cargo ships, the wooden wharf is now home to seafood restaurants and snack shacks, a touristy Mexican cantina, and a gaily colored turn-of-the-20th-century indoor wooden carousel (which Paul Newman operated in *The Sting*). A small amusement area perched halfway down, **Pacific Park** (⌀ **310/260-8744;** www.pacpark.com), hearkens back to the granddaddy pier amusement park in California, Pacific Ocean Park; this updated version has a Ferris wheel, roller coaster, and other rides, right on the ocean's edge. Anglers head to the pier's end to fish, and nostalgia buffs to view the photographic display of the pier's history. This is the last of the great pleasure piers, offering rides, romance, and perfect panoramic views of the bay and mountains.

The fulcrum of a 60-mile beachfront stretching from celebrity-riddled Malibu to the Palos Verdes Peninsula, Santa Monica is prime real estate, with stylish oceanfront hotels, an artsy atmosphere, and somewhat wacky residents. We never come here without spending at least some time hanging out at the Third Street Promenade, a pedestrian-only outdoor mall lined with shops and restaurants; we dig the **Fatburger,** an outpost of a legendary Southern California fast-food chain. Might as well go for the total SoCal experience.

ⓘ **Visitor Information Center,** 1920 Main St., Ste. B (⌀ **800/544-5319** or 310/393-7593; www.santamonica.com)

✈ Los Angeles International

🛏 $ **Best Western Marina Pacific,** 1697 Pacific Ave., Venice (© **800/786-7789** or 310/452-1111; www.mphotel.com). $$$ **Hotel Oceana,** 849 Ocean Ave., Santa Monica (© **800/777-0758** or 310/393-0486; www.hoteloceanasantamonica.com).

WHY THEY'LL THANK YOU: Classic beach vibe.

Beaches **88**

Kauai: An Embarrassment of Riches

All ages • Kauai, Hawaii

WHEN IT COMES TO BEACHES, HAWAII HAS MORE BEAUTIES THAN ANY one state deserves; truth to tell, the garden isle of Kauai on its own has more stunning beaches than any state deserves. With its lush tropical greenery, soft golden sand, majestic ocean cliffs, and purposely low-key development—no building may exceed the height of a coconut palm—this island is a beach lover's dream.

I find it hard to resist the temptation of hanging out at popular **Hanalei Beach** on the North Coast—2 miles long, with relatively placid waters good for swimming, and all the restrooms and other beachfront facilities that are necessary when you've got kids with you. (And, I have to admit, I relish the opportunity to torture my children by singing "Puff, the Magic Dragon" over and over.) Sure, it's popular, with tourists and locals alike—you may have to walk a ways to find a spot to drop your towels—but in my experience, children *like* having other sunbathers around; making some new friends to help build sand forts is generally a plus. They don't place the same value on "getting away from it all" as we stressed-out adults (or canoodling honeymooners) do.

Still, for the best family beach on Kauai, my vote goes to **Poipu Beach,** on Kauai's sun-soaked south shore. Developed but not

Waimea Canyon, Kauai.

overdeveloped, the whole Poipu resort area offers the requisite amenities, but you'll never feel crowded the way you might at Oahu's Waikiki Beach. Big, wide Poipu Beach Park is the place to hit the golden sands, equipped with restrooms and showers, a picnic area and restaurant. You can easily plant yourselves for a full day without getting restless; the beach is incredibly versatile—head to the left of the sandbar and you find a calm, child-friendly sandy-bottom pool protected by a lava-rock jetty; head to the right and you face an open bay of vivid turquoise water that attracts swimmers, snorkelers, and surfers. The curling waves here are enough to hang ten, yet small enough to bodysurf or boogie-board. Poipu Beach is an excellent place to learn to surf; lessons are available from numerous local outfits, the oldest and best being **Margo Oberg's School of Surfing,** Nukumoi Surf Shop, across from Brennecke's Beach (✆ **808/332-6100;** www.surfonkauai.com). Snorkelers can rent gear from **Snorkel Bob's Kauai,** 3236 Poipu Rd. (✆ **808/742-2206**), which also rents boogie boards.

If you're looking for a break from the beach, explore what some have dubbed the Grand Canyon of the Pacific, **Waimea Canyon.** This valley, known for its reddish lava beds, reminds everyone who sees it of the Grand Canyon. Kauai's version is bursting with ever-changing color, just like its namesake, but it's smaller—only a mile wide, 3,567 feet deep, and 12 miles long. A massive earthquake sent streams into the single river that ultimately carved this picturesque canyon. Today, the Waimea River—a silver thread of water in the gorge that's sometimes a trickle, often a torrent, but always there—keeps cutting the canyon deeper and wider, and nobody can say what the result will be 100 million years from now.

ⓘ Hoone Rd., Koloa (www.poipu-beach.org)

✈ Lihue

🛏 $$$ **Hyatt Regency Kauai Resort,** 1571 Poipu Rd. (📞 **800/55-HYATT** or 808/742-1234; www.kauai-hyatt.com). $ **Kalaheo Inn,** 4444 Papalina Rd. (📞 **888/332-6023** or 808/332-6023; www.kalaheoinn.com).

WHY THEY'LL THANK YOU: Riding that first wave.

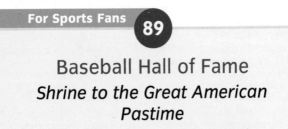

For Sports Fans 89

Baseball Hall of Fame
Shrine to the Great American Pastime
Ages 6 & up • Cooperstown, New York

ADMITTEDLY MY FAMILY IS CRAZY FOR BASEBALL, BUT EVEN WHEN I look at it objectively, I'd have to say that the Baseball Hall of Fame in Cooperstown sets the gold standard for sports museums. The very word *Cooperstown* has become synonymous with baseball history, for legend (now discredited) claims that Abner Doubleday invented baseball here. Opened in 1939, the Hall of Fame has been around long enough to amass an unparalleled collection of sports memorabilia. You don't have to be a statistic-spouting baseball fanatic to feel moved by this homage to America's pastime.

The Hall's red-brick Federal-style facade looks as all-American as the game it represents. Laid down like a giant timeline, it walks you through the **history of baseball,** starting with the various European ball-and-bat games that were its predecessors. Recent renovations have added more hands-on and interactive exhibits for kids, including a 13-minute multimedia show and a special area for toddlers and preschoolers, but it's the **memorabilia** that really tells the story, from Ty Cobb's glove to Babe Ruth's bat. You'll see the ridiculous scanty protective gear catchers used to

Ty Cobb's plaque at the Baseball Hall of Fame.

wear behind the plate, the gradual evolution of the regulation ball and bat, a panoply of uniforms through the decades, the ever-changing look of trading cards. You'll learn about the Black Sox scandal of 1919 and how baseball survived World War II. Special galleries are devoted to topics such as the Negro Leagues and the women's professional leagues. Snippets of vintage broadcasts and video footage of historic games are played at the touch of a button. Sure, my kids gravitated at first to exhibits paying tribute to today's stars and teams, set in a replica major-league locker room, but the more they saw of baseball's storied past—the actual objects, worn and discolored from play—the more they got into it. We saved a stroll through the actual Hall of Fame gallery for last, and by that time, those names on the plaques really meant something.

(i) 25 Main St. ((C) **888/HALL-OF-FAME** or 607/547-7200; http://
web.baseballhalloffame.org)

✈ Albany, 75 miles

🛏 $ **Best Western,** 50 Commons Dr. ((C) **607/547-7100;** www.
bwcooperstown.com). $$$ **Inn at Cooperstown,** 16 Chestnut St.
((C) **607/547-5756;** www.innatcooperstown.com).

WHY THEY'LL THANK YOU: Baseball is more than a game, it's a
window on America.

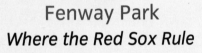

For Sports Fans

90

Fenway Park
Where the Red Sox Rule
Ages 6 & up • Boston, Massachusetts

WHEN THE **BOSTON RED SOX** WON THE 2004 WORLD SERIES—ENDING
an 86-year dry spell—they may have lost their status as one of base-
ball's most beloved underdogs, but I haven't heard any members of
Red Sox Nation complaining. Sure, the Yankees, their perennial
American League East rivals down in New York City, have a higher
payroll and more world titles. None of that matters to dedicated Red
Sox supporters, and their numbers are legion. The 2005 movie *Fever
Pitch* didn't exaggerate anything: Sit among them in the stands and
you'll definitely remember that the word "fan" comes from "fanatic."
But I for one never mind. You're watching ball in an intensely green
place that's older than your grandparents, inhaling a Fenway Frank
and wishing for a home run—what could be better?

My father was a Red Sox true believer his whole life, and though my
family has committed the ultimate treason of rooting for the Yan-
kees, we still harbor a secret fondness for the Sox. So it is that from
time to time, we take off our Yankees caps and visit Fenway Park.

A night game at Fenway Park.

It's a venerable stadium, though "stadium" seems almost too grand a term for this, the oldest park in the major leagues (built in 1912). Its quirks only add to the Fenway mystique: the narrow seats, the hand-operated scoreboard, the 37-foot-high left-field wall known as the **"Green Monster"** for its tendency to rob opposing hitters of their home runs. Those seats may be uncomfortable but they're gratifyingly close to the field, without the wide swaths of grass other parks have put between the fans and the players.

Compared with its modern brethren, however, Fenway is tiny, and **tickets** are both expensive and hard to get. Throughout the season, a limited number of standing-room tickets go on sale the day of the game, and fans sometimes return presold tickets (especially if a rainout causes rescheduling). It can't hurt to check. Forced to choose between seats in a low-numbered grandstand section—say, 10 or below—and those in the bleachers, go for the bleachers. They can get rowdy during night games, but the view is better from there than from the deep right-field corner.

We took a **Fenway Park tour** (conducted year-round; no tours on game days or holidays) that actually allowed us to peer inside the cramped space behind the Green Monster and walk out onto the warning track, stop in the press box, and visit the Red Sox Hall of Fame. Best of all, the guide's commentary was rich in team lore and highly entertaining.

(i) 4 Yawkey Way (© **877/REDSOX-9** for tickets, 617/226-6666 for tours; www.redsox.com)

✈ ⊨ See Boston Common ⑯.

BEST TIME: Season runs Apr–Oct.

WHY THEY'LL THANK YOU: Baseball legends still matter here.

For Sports Fans

91

Wrigley Field: The Cubs' Den
Ages 4 & up • Chicago, Illinois

THE CHICAGO CUBS HAVEN'T PLAYED IN THE WORLD SERIES SINCE 1945 and haven't won the darn thing since 1908—when the Red Sox finally won a Series in 2004, the Cubs became undisputed holders of the crown for Most Beloved Losers. Chicagoans do love their Cubbies, champs or not, and there's no question that the team plays in one of baseball's classic venues, tiny Wrigley Field. Back in 1988 lights were finally installed for night play, but they're rarely used—the Cubs still play mostly day games. With its ivy-covered outfield walls, a hand-operated scoreboard, a view of Lake Michigan from the upper deck, and the El rattling past, it's old-fashioned baseball all the way, and our kids enjoyed every minute of their game there.

Built in 1914, Wrigley Field is the second-oldest venue in baseball (after **Fenway Park 90**), although the Cubs didn't move in until 1916 (a decade after their last Series victory!). Originally Weeghman Field, it was renamed in 1926 after the team's new owner, William Wrigley, Jr., the chewing-gum magnate.

No matter how the Cubs are doing in the standings, tickets go fast—most weekend and night games are sold out by Memorial Day. Your best bet is to hit a weekday game, where you'll be sitting alongside plenty of Chicagoans who called in sick to work and miraculously recovered by game time. Wrigley is small enough that every seat is a decent seat, and the place truly earns its nickname "The Friendly Confines"—every time I've been there, the fans around me were passionate, friendly, well-informed, and good-natured in the face of defeat. Riding the Red Line El to the Addison Street stop is part of the experience: You can look down into the park from the train, and hear the roar of the crowd as soon as you step onto the platform. During the regular season on non–game days, you can take a 90-minute **tour** of the vintage stadium, visiting the press box, dugouts, both visitors' and Cubs' clubhouses, and the playing field itself; these tours are popular, so book in advance (℡ **773/404-CUBS**).

Just some of the **traditions** we love at Wrigley: Enterprising owners of surrounding houses have built stands on their roofs where they seat their own ticket holders; ground rules declare that if a ball gets stuck in the ivy, it's a double; and a pennant is flown after every game with a big "w" or "l" to alert passersby to the outcome of the game (who needs the Internet?). When the opposing team hits a home run out of the park, somebody on the sidewalk outside picks up the offending ball and throws it back in. You've gotta love a ballpark where that happens.

ⓘ 1060 W. Addison St. (℡ **773/404-CUBS**; www.cubs.mlb.com)
✈ 🛏 See Chicago **15**.

WHY THEY'LL THANK YOU: Watching a Cubs homer sail over those ivy walls.

Notre Dame
The Holy Land of College Football

Ages 8 & up (Notre Dame), 6 & up (Hall of Fame) •
South Bend, Indiana

From Notre Dame Stadium, you can see a 132-foot-high mosaic of Jesus on the side wall of the campus library—a mosaic shrewdly placed so that Christ, with upraised hands, is centered right over the north goal post. **Touchdown Jesus** is a fitting sight for this Catholic university in northern Indiana, which has had no fewer than eight national championships, seven Heisman Trophy winners, five number-one pro draft picks, and 171 All-Americans. You don't have to be an alum to be a rabid fan of Notre Dame football—you just have to love football, like my teenage son does.

Notre Dame has had a football team since 1887 (though its famous marching band is even older, the oldest in the country, formed in 1845). The red-brick stadium is vintage, built in 1930, the last year of famed coach Knute Rockne's decade at the school. Rockne more than anyone is responsible for the nationwide Notre Dame fan base, for he actively sought far-flung matches and developed cross-country rivalries, with such schools as Michigan, USC, Navy, and Boston College. Notre Dame's popularity nowadays transcends regional loyalties; they're the nation's only football team, pro or collegiate, whose entire schedule is broadcast on radio coast to coast, and since 1966 there's only been one home game that wasn't sold out. But here's the catch: All 80,000 seats to home games are allocated to season ticket holders, alumni, students, faculty, and parents of current students, but somehow they do pop up on ticket services (at inflated prices, of course). Or work your connections—find a Notre Dame alum or parent who'll buy tickets for you. Otherwise, you'll have to be content with buying merchandise at the Irish Store in Eck Hall, or taking a 1¼-hour, free (on weekdays), student-led **walking tour** of the beautiful rolling campus (call ✆ **574/631-5726**), which doesn't go inside the stadium.

There is, however, another reason to come to South Bend. In 1995 the **College Football Hall of Fame** moved from King's Island, Ohio, to a new state-of-the-art facility in downtown South Bend. Built to look like a football stadium, with a green gridiron-lined outdoor plaza, the museum has, besides the honoree exhibits, plenty of interactive kiosks, a 360-degree theater where you can stand surrounded by the noisy blur of game-day action, and sizable interactive areas for testing your skills against some of the greatest players in college football history.

ⓘ **Notre Dame Stadium,** University of Notre Dame (www.und. collegesports.com). **College Football Hall of Fame,** 111 S. St. Joseph St. (ⓒ **800/440-FAME** or 574/235-9999; www.college football.org).

✈ South Bend Regional

🛏 $$ **Comfort Suites,** 52939 S.R. 933 N. (ⓒ **574/272-1500;** www.comfortsuites.com). $$ **Inn at St. Mary's,** 53993 U.S. Hwy. 933 (ⓒ **574/232-4000;** www.innatsaintmarys.com).

WHY THEY'LL THANK YOU: Seeing Touchdown Jesus.

93 For Sports Fans

The Kentucky Derby
Bluegrass & Red Roses
Ages 4 & up • Louisville, Kentucky

AS A KID, I MUST ADMIT BEING DISAPPOINTED THAT THE GRASS WASN'T bright blue in Kentucky bluegrass country, although it does have a bluish cast. Legend has it that this species of grass is the best for raising Thoroughbred racehorses. It must have some effect, because more than two-thirds of the winners of the Kentucky Derby—America's premier horse race—have been bred right here on Kentucky's splendid horse farms.

Louisville's **Churchill Downs** racetrack, its huge white frame grandstand topped by a distinctive pair of slim gray spires, opened in 1875, and the Kentucky Derby—originally patterned after England's Epsom Derby—has been run every May since then. It's the first in the Triple Crown, a trio of renowned flat races for 3-year-olds, and its traditions have become famous, from the prerace singing of "My Old Kentucky Home" down to the garland of 554 red roses draped over the winning colt's neck. Grandstand seats for the Derby must be booked months ahead and cost a fortune; a more casual option is to join the euphoric crowd picnicking in the 40-acre infield (you won't see much of the race but you'll have a fun party).

The **Kentucky Derby Museum,** open year-round just outside Gate #1 (© 502/637-1111), has videos and hands-on exhibits (don't miss the one where you sit on a saddle in a real starting gate).

Before you hit the track, though, I suggest driving around the countryside near Lexington, 100 miles southeast of Louisville, to see where generations of Thoroughbred champions have been bred. The most famous horse farm, **Calumet Farms,** doesn't allow visitors, though you can do a drive-by with Horse Farm Tours (© 859/268-2906), which then visits other working horse farms. You can tour **Claiborne Farm,** Winchester Road, Paris (© 859/233-4252), where Seabiscuit was born and Secretariat was a longtime stud stallion (his grave is on the farm), or **Three Chimneys Farm,** Old Frankfort Parkway, Versailles (© 859/873-7053), where Seattle Slew was the resident stud. The **Kentucky Horse Park,** 4089 Iron Works Pike, Lexington (© 800/568-8813 or 859/233-4303; www.kyhorsepark.com), has Man O' War's grave and a museum on horse history, but kids really have more fun walking through the barns, seeing shows in the equestrian arena (mid-Mar to Oct), and taking horse and pony rides.

ⓘ 700 Central Ave. (© **502/636-4400;** www.churchilldowns.com)

✈ Louisville International

🛏 $$$ **Seelbach Hilton,** 500 4th St., Louisville (© **502/585-3200;** www.seelbachhilton.com). $$ **Doubletree Guest Suites Lexington,** 2601 Richmond Rd., Lexington (© **800/262-3774** or 859/268-0060; www.doubletree.com).

WHY THEY'LL THANK YOU: And they're off!

International Tennis Hall of Fame
Where Newport's New Sport Became King

Ages 6 & up • Newport, Rhode Island

MIFFED AT FELLOW MEMBERS OF NEWPORT'S EXCLUSIVE NEWPORT Reading Room club, in 1880 *New York Herald* publisher James Gordon Bennett, Jr., launched a rival club called the Newport Casino. Determined to make it bigger, better, and more fashionable, Bennett hired McKim Mead & White—favorite architects of the Gilded Age New York elite—to produce a rambling shingle-style edifice of lavish proportions, with dark-green turrets and verandas and an interior piazza for games and social events. Along with archery and lawn bowling, space was provided for a new game called lawn tennis, which quickly took root among upper-class athletes. The very next year, the newly formed US Lawn Tennis Association held its first national championship at the Casino's grass **Horseshoe Court.** Now known as the US Open, this tournament is played at Flushing Meadows, Queens, but the Casino still holds professional tournaments, as well as the U.S. amateur grass championship. The Horseshoe Court is a permanent grass court, one of few remaining in this hard-court age, and there's still a **walled court** for court tennis, one of only nine in the United States. And in the elegant former club rooms, the old Casino has, since 1954, housed the **International Tennis Hall of Fame.**

Even if you're not a die-hard tennis fan, it's fun to tour the Hall of Fame just to explore this landmark building. Exhibits explore how lawn tennis exploded in popu-larity, how professional tennis developed out of the amateur sport, and the growth of women's tennis. Honorees include American champions from Bill Tilden and Stan Smith to John McEnroe, Jimmy Connors, Billie Jean King, and Chris Evert, not to mention the African-American groundbreakers Althea Gibson and Arthur Ashe. The Hall of Fame doesn't play

The Tennis Hall of Fame.

national favorites; you'll see plaques for such international talents as France's Rene Lacoste and Yannick Noah; Sweden's Bjorn Borg and Mats Wilander; Germany's Steffi Graf and Boris Becker; Australia's John Newcombe and Evonne Goolagong; Romania's Ilie Nastase; Argentina's Guillermo Vilas; and Czechslovakia's Martina Navratilova. Even a kid who's just picked up a racquet can feel swept into a grand old sporting tradition here.

(i) 194 Bellevue Ave. ((C) **800/457-1144** or 401/849-3990; www. tennisfame.com)

✈ 🛏 See Newport's Mansions **71**.

WHY THEY'LL THANK YOU: How a pastime of the privileged became a sport of the people.

For Sports Fans **95**

NASCAR Classic: The Daytona 500

Ages 4 & up • Daytona, Florida

Like much else in Florida, it all began with a beach: beautiful Daytona Beach, which runs for 24 miles along a skinny peninsula divided from the north Florida mainland by the Halifax River. In the early 1900s, when "horseless carriages" were still a novelty, automobile enthusiasts discovered that Daytona Beach's uniquely hard-packed white sand made the perfect drag strip. A century later, the town has every right to call itself "The World Center of Racing."

Auto racing in Daytona outgrew the beach long ago. In 1959, a proper 2¹/₂-mile racetrack, the **Daytona International Speedway,** was built 4 miles inland, and stock car racing's premier event, the 200-lap Daytona 500, was launched. The National Association for Stock Car Auto Racing (NASCAR) is now based in Daytona, and over a million race fans come here for 9 or 10 major events a year. Big races sell out months in advance—tickets to the Daytona 500 in February can be gone a year ahead of time (✆ **386/253-7223** for tickets).

If you're not attending a race, you can still get a fair idea by visiting the **World Center of Racing Visitor Center** at the east end of the speedway. You can enter the stands to see the track, or take a 30-minute **guided tram tour** that visits the garage area, pit road, and so on. Speed freaks can pay a stiff fee to have the **Richard Petty Driving Experience,** run by seven-time Daytona 500 winner Richard Petty (✆ **800/237-3889;** www.1800bepetty.com; May–Oct)—a three-lap ride around the tri-oval track in a real stock car, cruising at an average speed of, oh, say 115 mph. The kids, however, may prefer to spend your money on the phenomenally popular **DAYTONA USA** (✆ **386/681-6800** or 386/681-6530; www.daytonausa. com), also in the visitor center, where all sorts of state-of-the-art motion simulators, interactive activities, and IMAX films re-create the adrenaline-pumping experience of racing in Daytona.

ⓘ 1801 W. International Speedway Blvd. (✆ **386/947-6866;** www. daytonaintlspeedway.com)

✈ Daytona Beach International

🛏 $$ **Shoreline All Suites Inn & Cabana Colony Cottages,** 2435 S. Atlantic Ave., Daytona Beach Shores (✆ **800/293-0653** or 386/252-1692; www.daytonashoreline.com)

WHY THEY'LL THANK YOU: Banking the turn into the home stretch.

The Call of the Wild in Denali
Your Own Personal Iditarod
Ages 10 & up • Denali National Park, Alaska

Alaska's Denali National Park is about as pristine a wilderness as a national park can get, and in an attempt to keep it that way, the Parks Service permits no public access by automobile—there's only one gravel road through the center of the park, which you can travel on a shuttle bus that links rest stops and campgrounds and lodges and scenic overlooks. Disembarking at various points, park-goers can then hike into the tundra as far as they wish, though most folks seem content just to ride the bus and look out the window at those incredible Arctic views. But there's another way to

Denali National Park.

get even deeper into this stunning wilderness—by racing over the snowy backcountry on a **dog sled,** just as the park rangers do.

Two outfits have been approved to run wintertime dog-sledding packages into Denali, using their own rustic lodges as home base (guests sleep in private log cabins near the lodges). Both of these lodges are just outside the park, but so close that they feature views of majestic Mount McKinley, America's biggest mountain. **Denali West Lodge,** set on the shore of Lake Minchumina, is the smaller of the two operations (only 10 guests at a time), and so remote that you'll need to fly in on a little private plane. Its mushing expeditions are mostly day trips from the lodge. You can drive via Alaska Hwy. 3 to **Earthsong Lodge,** which runs 3- to 10-day dog-sledding camp-outs (using tents or outlying cabins), although itineraries can be tailored to guests' interests. Each guest 12 and over drives his or her own sled, with teams of four to six huskies. (Younger children may simply ride along on the sled.) Earthsong even offers an option for summer visitors to get a taste of the dog-sledding experience by driving a husky team with a wheeled cart.

It may sound as if you'd need special skills, but the proprietors of both lodges are longtime mushers experienced in training first-timers. You just need to be strong enough to hold on tight as the dogs surge forward, whipping you over the snowy track. Perhaps 4 or 5 hours of the day is spent mushing, covering on average 30 miles of terrain, across the snowy tundra, around lakes, through taiga forests and glacial river valleys. You're practically guaranteed sightings of moose, caribou, Dall sheep, foxes, lynx, wolverines, and beavers; your chances of running across other human beings, however, are practically nil. Nighttime camp-outs may be lit by the Northern Lights and serenaded by nearby wolves, howling in sync with the huskies. Now *that's* getting away from it all.

ⓘ Denali Park Rd. (📞 **907/683-2294;** www.nps.gov/dena)

✈ Fairbanks, 125 miles. Anchorage, 236 miles.

🚂 **Alaska Railroad** (📞 **800/544-0552** or 907/265-2494; www.alaskarailroad.com) runs trains from Anchorage (6½ hr.) and from Fairbanks (3¾ hr.) summers only.

🛏 $$$ **Denali West Lodge** (📞 **907/674-3112;** www.denali westlodge.com). $$$ **Earthsong Lodge** (📞 **907/683-2863;** www. earthsonglodge.com).

BEST TIME: Nov–Mar.

WHY THEY'LL THANK YOU: Bonding with the huskies.

Roller Coasters   **97**

The Cyclone

The Coaster That Made Coney Island Famous

Ages 8 & up • Brooklyn, New York

BACK IN THE DAYS BEFORE AIR-CONDITIONING, NEW YORK FAMILIES flocked to the beach at Coney Island to cool off in summer, and it was a rite of passage to grow tall enough (54 in.) to be allowed on New York's most famous roller coaster, The Cyclone. Thrill rides may have advanced technologically since then, but this classic coaster, built in 1927, is still one of the best, plunging a heart-stopping eight stories from its highest peak.

The charms of Coney Island go well beyond the Cyclone, of course; for one thing, there's that dynamite location, right on a wide white-sand beach where Atlantic waters crash. **The New York Aquarium,** Surf Avenue and West 8th Street (📞 **718/265-3400;** www. nyaquarium.com), just a short stroll up the boardwalk, features dolphins, sea lions, seals, and walruses. Also clustering along the boardwalk are a handful of small private amusement parks, each selling their own ride tickets. At 12th Street, Demo's Wonder Wheel Park features the 1920 landmark **Wonder Wheel,** an ingenious double Ferris wheel of gargantuan proportions. For those who like to stay closer to earth, there are bumper cars, tilt-a-whirls, spinning teacups, carousels, and kiddie rides, as well as satisfyingly cheesy arcades; the area also has mini-golf and go-kart concessions.

Coney Island's Wonder Wheel.

Compared to huge plasticized theme parks like Disney, Six Flags, and Busch Gardens, the Coney Island amusements have a grungy midway glamour that older kids will appreciate—it's the Real Thing. (With kids, it's best to visit by day—and know where your wallet is at all times.)

The beach and boardwalk have been spruced up lately, though, and the beachfront souvenir shops and food stands have acquired a post-modern hipster gloss, with Brooklyn artists decorating their side walls with retro murals. Even the local freak show, tucked up a Surf Avenue side street near the parks, has the whiff of a performance art installation. The Stillwell Avenue subway station (last stop for the D and F trains) has been refurbished to a high sheen, and along the boardwalk to the east, there's a tidy baseball stadium for a popular Mets farm team, the **Brooklyn Cyclones** (© **718/449-8497;** www.brooklyncyclones.com). But you can still get a reliable kosher frank at Nathan's famous open-air hot dog stand on Surf Avenue—some things never change.

(i) Surf Avenue and W. 10th St. ((C) **718/372-0275;** www.astroland. com)

✈ 🛏 See Manhattan **14**.

BEST TIME: Amusement parks open daily June to Labor Day, weekends Apr–May and Sept–Oct.

WHY THEY'LL THANK YOU: Atmosphere, atmosphere, atmosphere.

Roller Coasters **98**

Millennium Force
Cedar Point's Record Setter
Ages 10 & up • Sandusky, Ohio

WHEN IT OPENED IN 2000, THE MILLENNIUM FORCE AT OHIO'S CEDAR Point amusement park not only was the world's tallest roller coaster (310 ft.), but also had the longest drop (300 ft.), the steepest banked turns of any noninverted coaster (122 degrees), and traveled at the fastest speed (93 mph). It may climb up that 310-foot peak (taller than the Statue of Liberty) at a modest 45-degree angle, but when it plunges down the other side it's angled at 80 degrees. It whips through two tunnels, and covers more than a mile in length, speeding to its finish line in 2 minutes and 20 seconds, almost before you know what hit you. But no record is unbreakable. Within 3 years, the Millennium Force was surpassed—by another roller coaster at Cedar Point, of course.

There's no question that Cedar Point prides itself on its roller coasters—it has 16 of them, the newest being the **Top Thrill Dragster,** which debuted in 2003. Top Thrill accelerates like a dragster

The Top Thrill Dragster at Cedar Point.

right out of the gate, taking only 4 seconds to reach 120 mph, then climbs *straight up,* perpendicular to the ground, to a height of 420 ft., the equivalent of a 42-story building. And what does it do next? It drops down just as steeply (again at 120 mph), throwing in a wrenching 270-degree twist. The **Wicked Twister** is another heart-in-your-mouth experience, a U-shaped suspended coaster that ping-pongs back and forth between two 215-foot-high towers, corkscrewing up and down each tower, three times forward and twice backward, reaching a speed of up to 70 mph. No wonder these two have a minimum height requirement of 52 inches, whereas for Millennium Force you only need to be 48 inches. Each of these coasters has its rabid fans, while others are passionate about the experience on **Magnum,** or **Raptor,** or **Gemini,** or **Blue Streak,** or any of the other innovative steel coasters at Cedar Point.

Like Lake Compounce above, Cedar Point is a vintage park, first opening in 1870 on a peninsula jutting out into Lake Erie, about halfway between Cleveland and Toledo. Cedar Point has 68 rides in all and that's not even counting the attractions at the adjoining 18-acre water park, **Soak City;** an indoor water park, **Castaway Island,** recently opened to extend the season (the outdoor areas are only open May to early Sept). Four resort hotels on the 364-acre property are available for those who need more than 1 day to do all the rides.

ⓘ 1 Cedar Point Dr. (ⓒ **419/627-2350;** www.cedarpoint.com)

✈ ⊨ See the Rock 'n' Roll Hall of Fame ❻❾.

BEST TIME: May to early Sept.

WHY THEY'LL THANK YOU: That moment at the peak, before the drop. Multiplied 16 times.

99

The Santa Cruz Boardwalk
California Classic by the Sea
All ages • Coast between Monterey & San Francisco, California

ONE OF THE FEW OLD-FASHIONED AMUSEMENT PARKS LEFT IN THE WORLD, the Santa Cruz Beach Boardwalk is California's answer to Rye Playland. Situated next to Santa Cruz's lovely mile-long public beach, the boardwalk is a half-mile strip of rides, shops, and restaurants, harking back to an era of seaside innocent fun. It's the sort of classic site you don't necessarily expect on the West Coast.

The park has 34 rides, two of them national landmarks. **The Carousel of Delight,** built in 1911 by Charles I.D. Looff, boasts hand-carved wooden horses, a 342-pipe organ band, and one of the few brass ring grabs left in existence; snatch the brass ring as your horse whirls past the post, then throw it into a painted clown's mouth to win a free ride. Looff's son, Arthur Looff, designed the park's other landmark, the red-and-white 1924 **Giant Dipper** roller coaster, which offers great views of Monterey Bay from its peaks—though few riders manage to take them in while being hurtled up and down at 55 mph. They have a split second longer to enjoy the views from the top of the 125-foot-tall Double Shot drop tower. A host of other thrill rides trade on speed, with names like Hurricane, Typhoon, and Tsunami; indoor "dark rides" include the Haunted Castle and Ghost Blaster, though I prefer the 1961-vintage **Cave Train,** where glow-in-the-dark prehistoric characters pop out. There is a section of smaller-scale rides for the under-36-inch crowd as well.

   Although there's no admission fee to get onto the boardwalk, the individual ride tickets can mount up fast—an "unlimited rides"

Santa Cruz Boardwalk.

bracelet, which at first doesn't seem cheap, could end up saving you money. The beach boardwalk keeps seasonal hours, open daily from Memorial Day weekend to Labor Day but only on weekends and holidays throughout the spring and fall.

ⓘ ℂ **831/423-5590;** www.beachboardwalk.com

✈ San Francisco International, 77 miles

🛏 $$ **Fern River Resort,** 5250 Hwy. 9, Felton (ℂ **831/335-4412;** www.fernriver.com)

WHY THEY'LL THANK YOU: Screaming from the top of the Giant Dipper.

The Mall of America
Minnesota's Mega-Mall Amusements
All ages • Bloomington, Minnesota

WHAT NERVE IT TOOK TO BUILD A SHOPPING CENTER IN SUBURBAN Minnesota and call it the Mall of America. And yet there is something iconic about this over-the-top shrine to consumerism. Subscribing to the all-American bigger-is-better philosophy, the mall could hold seven Yankee Stadiums or 258 Statues of Liberty; walk one circuit around a level of stores and you've clocked nearly a mile. There are over 520 stores at this huge retail center 20 minutes south of downtown Minneapolis, stacked on four brightly lit levels around a central glass atrium—not only that, but 14 movie screens, a food court, 20 sit-down restaurants, half a dozen attractions, and even a wedding chapel. You've got to see it to believe it.

The main attraction is **Camp Snoopy,** America's largest enclosed theme park, which covers 7 ground-floor acres in the immense central atrium with 30 rides, including a kiddie roller coaster that loops around large planters full of trees. This will thrill toddlers and young grade schoolers; kids who've outgrown those tame rides will still enjoy the **Underwater Adventures Aquarium,** where 4,500 sea creatures swim around in tanks on a subterranean level. Between the virtual submarine ride and the "shark encounter"—a glass tunnel that walks you through a shark tank—it's like a mini–Sea World. At the *mall.*

For teens or preteens (and, admit it, adults too), the **A.C.E.S Flight Simulators** let you play virtual pilot on an F-18 Hornet jet or a WWII-era P-51 Mustang. An even bigger deal is the **NASCAR Silicon Motor Speedway,** where anyone over 52 inches tall can get behind the wheel of a rigged-up stationary stock car and spend 20 minutes stepping on the gas, banking on the turns, and stomping on the brakes (there's a passenger seat where kids age 4 and older can ride shotgun on this virtual race).

While not strictly a theme attraction (no admission charge, for one thing), the four-story **Lego store** is as good as a ride, with some 90 life-size Lego models to marvel at; the **Build-a-Bear Workshop** is another store that offers plenty of entertainment. So what if most of the other shops are the usual gang of chain stores? It's called the Mall of America, dude—so who's expecting snooty high-end retail? It's supersize, it's commercial, and it caters to the masses—and there's nothing more American than that.

(i) 60 E. Broadway (www.mallofamerica.com)

✈ Minneapolis/St. Paul International, 10 miles

🛏 $ **Best Western Kelly Inn,** 161 Saint Anthony Ave., St. Paul (© **800/WESTERN** or 651/227-8711; www.bestwestern.com). $$ **Doubletree Park Place,** 1500 Park Place Blvd., Minneapolis (© **800/ 222-TREE** or 952/542-8600; www.doubletree.com).

WHY THEY'LL THANK YOU: Looking down from Level 4 to see Camp Snoopy below.

Indexes

General Index

INDEX

Geographical Index

Photo Credits